"But in your hearts set apart Christ as Lord. Always be prepared to give an answer to everyone who asks you to give the reason for the hope that you have. But do this with gentleness and respect"

1 Peter 3:15

The BEST FACTS: Apologetics for Every Believer

"Do you wonder what to say in presenting the Gospel facts? Or perhaps you are concerned about a difficult objection? The Best Facts is a helpful volume to assist believers in doing precisely these things—both utilizing good support for Christianity as well as addressing those common objections. Both explanations as well as easy-to-learn lists of talking points in the appendices allow quick recall. Witnessing with confidence is the goal here and this text has done the hard work for you." - **Dr. Gary R. Habermas**, Distinguished Research Professor & Chair, Philosophy Dept., Liberty University.

The **BEST FACTS** and **TALL TALES** acronyms were designed to help you memorize a coherent defense of your faith. Please commit these acronyms to memory and try to learn the arguments we'll go over in this workbook. This will equip you to silence doubt when you encounter it, encourage doubting believers when you encounter them, and answer honest questions from non-believers when you encounter them. We hope this resource will equip you to walk confidently with God and to share your faith boldly.

Contents

Preface

Thank you so much for picking up this copy of the BEST FACTS workbook. I am confident that this resource will equip you to confidently deal with doubt and defend your faith. This resource is a very basic introduction to Christian apologetics that has been put together in order to equip you to coherently defend your faith.

For years, Christians would come to me and say, "I talked with a skeptic and told them they should come talk to you about the evidence for Christianity." After hearing statements like that for years but never once having a single one of their skeptical friends follow through and find me to speak more, I decided it was time to equip each of those friends to coherently defend their faith.

There are countless other good apologetical resources. What this workbook will do is unique. This workbook will be a short, simple, broad, and easy to remember book on apologetics. It will equip you with an easy to remember set of acronyms, the BEST FACTS and TALL TALES acronyms, that will give you a coherent framework for a robust defense of your faith.

We hope you'll memorize these acronyms and arguments and use what you learn in this book to respectfully defend your faith and to confidently deal with doubt. Thanks so much for reading this book!

Nate Herbst, 7/21/17

1
An Introduction to Apologetics

An Introduction to Apologetics.

In Mark 12:30, Jesus said the greatest commandment was to love "God with all your heart, and with all your soul, and with all your mind, and with all your strength." The idea of leaving your brain at the door to follow God is not a Christian one. Growing in the area of apologetics is one way to grow closer to God and it is a valuable skill for reaching others for Christ as well.

1 Peter 3:15 says, "But in your hearts set apart Christ as Lord. Always be prepared to give an answer to everyone who asks you to give the reason for the hope that you have. But do this with gentleness and respect."

The word translated here as "give the reason" is the Greek word ἀπολογία, or Aplogia, which means "to give a defense." This is the word that apologetics comes from. Apologetics involves giving a coherent defense of the Christian faith in a respectful way.

1 Peter 3:15 gives us five keys for defending our faith. These are 1) Relinquish control, 2) Resolve to be a light, 3) Ready yourself, 4) Reach out, and 5) Respect those you share with.

Key 1: Relinquish control - "But in your hearts set apart Christ as Lord"

In Matt. 28:18-20, Jesus said, "All authority in heaven and on earth has been given to me. Therefore go and make disciples of all nations, baptizing them in the name of the Father and of the Son and of the Holy Spirit, and teaching them to obey everything I have commanded you. And surely I am with you always, to the very end of the age."

How do you need to relinquish control so God can use you?

Decide to surrender to Him so He can work in and through you.

Key 2: Resolve to be a light - "But in your hearts set apart Christ as Lord"

Jesus called believers to be a light in this dark world (Matt. 5:14). He has strategically placed you in a specific time and place for that reason (Acts. 17:26-27).

People need to hear the Gospel (Rom. 10:13-14). Choose to be a light that shines brightly in this dark world.

Key 3: Ready yourself - "Always be prepared..."

God calls us to be ambassadors who are committed to persuading people of the truth of the Gospel (2 Cor. 5:11-21). Paul "persuaded" people to follow Christ in Thessalonica, Athens, Corinth, Ephesus, Caesarea, and Rome (Acts 17:2, 4, 17, 18:4, 19, 19:26, 24:25, 28:23). Unconvinced apologists are unconvincing (and there are too many of those). It is critical that we diligently prepare to persuade others.

How do you need to grow in the area of apologetics?

The BEST FACTS and TALL TALES acronyms will equip you to do this. Commit to learning them.

Key 4: Reach out - "Always be prepared to give an answer to everyone who asks you to give the reason for the hope that you have."

People can't ask you about a hope they don't know you have. It is critical that we take the initiative to reach out to others, believing that the harvest is very ripe (Matt. 9:37-38).

People really are lost and need Jesus. He is the only hope of salvation and the only answer to humanity's problems. People need Him. Unfortunately, many have a warped view of God and countless people are ignorant of the evidence for the Christian faith. We must be diligent to reach them!

Key 5: Respect those you share with - "But do this with gentleness and respect..."

Embrace Jesus' compassionate heart for the harvest (Matt. 9:36). Don't win an argument at the expense of a soul.

How can you be more respectful in defending your faith?

With the biblical call to apologetics in mind, let's turn to the BEST FACTS.

The BEST acronym

The BEST acronym describes some of the strong evidence for the existence of God. Of course, there is much more evidence for God's existence than could possibly be discussed here but these four arguments are a great start. Get more on each below.

B - The Beginning of the Universe Points to God: This has traditionally been called the "Cosmological Argument" for God's existence. Logic dictates and science corroborates a supernatural beginning of the universe out of nothing a finite time ago. Some might call it the "Big Bang" but we know it's what the Bible calls creation.

Both the beginning of the universe and the beginning of life point to God.

E - The Engineering of the Universe Points to God: This has traditionally been called the "Teleological Argument" for God's existence. There are countless constants and parameters of the universe that must be exactly right for life to be possible on earth. Similarly, information is programmed into every component of the universe. This "fine-tuning" of the universe is evidence of an all powerful and good creator of life. This is a compelling argument for God's existence.

S - Standards and Morality Point to God: This has traditionally been called the "Moral Argument" for God's existence. We all know some things are right (ex. Love) while others are wrong (ex. Hate). Objective morality can only be true if an objective moral law giver and enforcer (i.e. God) exists. If not, anything literally goes. We know anything doesn't go so we know God exists. If you believe in objective morality, you agree God must exist.

T - The Truth About Jesus Points to God: The gospel accounts are trustworthy and corroborated by history. The evidence for his life, death and resurrection is overwhelming. The evidence for the resurrection is particularly irrefutable. You should commit this evidence to memory and use it often. As C.S. Lewis states, Jesus was either a liar, lunatic or Lord and God. The evidence supports the latter! We can trust Him and the Bible He affirmed. That leads us to the validity of scripture.

The FACTS acronym

The FACTS acronym will help you remember some of the evidence for faith in Jesus and the Bible specifically. Once again, there is much more evidence than could possibly be explained here but this is a great start. The acronym below will equip you to defend your Christian faith and the reliability of the Bible.

F - The Bible Foretells the Future: Several hundred Biblical prophecies have been accurately fulfilled with more being fulfilled in modern times. This is conclusive evidence of God's fingerprints on scripture. Jesus alone fulfilled more than 100 prophecies. There is no natural way to explain this away.

A - The Bible is Archeologically Accurate: It has been said that no archeological find has ever disproved the Bible. The Bible is historically accurate as God's Word must be. Many archeological finds continue to affirm the trustworthiness of the Bible. The Bible's accurate history requires that it be treated with respect.

C – The Bible is Coherent: The Bible is coherent and contradiction free. The Bible corresponds with reality. Much has been made of the supposed contradictions in the Bible but these are easily cleared up with careful analysis. Most of these supposed contradictions arise due to our modern misunderstanding of the text. There are good answers for any contradictions the skeptic might bring up.

T - The Bible has been Translated Correctly: We've all heard the statement that you can't trust the Bible because it has been translated too many times. People often try to equate the Bible with the "telephone game" not realizing the Bible's reliability. The attacks are unfounded. There are many early manuscripts allowing us to know for certain what was written. The New Testament has been described as the most reliable ancient text. You can and should trust it!

S - The Bible has Scientific Statements: The Bible is not a science textbook but its numerous scientific pronouncements show yet again the fingerprints of God. The beginning of the universe (Gen. 1:1), the expansion of the universe (Ps. 104:2 and more), entropy, the second law of thermodynamics (Ps. 102:26, Heb. 1:11 and more), general relativity (Ps. 90:4, 2 Peter 3:8), radioactive decay (2 Peter 3:10), and other scientific realities were written in scripture thousands of years before science caught up. The skeptic can't just ignore these.

Which of the BEST FACTS stuck out to young why?

Notes to remember

Ask good questions and listen carefully. Ask more good questions. Be aware of peoples' presuppositions. Many presuppositions will guide people's worldviews. Look deeper than the surface level argument to see what's really happening. Stay smart.

Watch out for bad arguments (ex. assuming metaphysical naturalism). Avoid using bad arguments as well! Don't wing it, study!

Be positive: Positive apologetics (defending your faith) and negative apologetics (refuting other worldviews) are both useful in different times and places. Try to keep 80% of your approach on the positive side of that spectrum. For positive apologetics (defending your faith), use the BEST FACTS acronym. For negative apologetics (refuting other worldviews), use the TALL TALES acronym. As far as being positive, stay respectful and friendly in your conversations as well.

Stay on track: Don't get sidetracked by minor issues but stay focused on major ones. Don't fight battles you can't win at the expense of ones you can't loose. Christians often focus their apologetics on things that are not fundamental to our faith, like the age of the earth (more on the related topic of evolution in lesson 12), and neglect to emphasize things that are fundamental to our faith and solidly supported by the evidence (for example, the resurrection, more on that in lesson 5). Ravi Zacharias explains it this way, "Rather than spend our time debating for hours whether its billions of years or whether its thousands of years, we should instead be arguing for the fact that you cannot explain the full questions of life - origin, meaning, morality and destiny - without a personal, moral, First Cause, which is God himself."[1] Keep your apologetics focused on the big issues that are critical to our faith.

Why is it important to keep apologetics Jesus-focused?

Finally, as you engage in apologetics, don't forget to cultivate the other areas of your walk with God as well. Remember, Jesus said to love God with all your heart, soul, and strength as well. Apologetics should be a vibrant part of your walk with God but it shouldn't ever be the extent of your relationship with Jesus.

Conclusion

When you encounter doubt, tell yourself the truth. Use the BEST FACTS and TALL TALES acronyms to remind yourself of the truth of our faith. When you share your faith, be respectful and be prepared to give good answers to honest questions. The BEST FACTS and TALL TALES acronyms will prepare you for that so memorize these acronyms. Keep your apologetics focused on the big issues that are fundamental to belief in Jesus and save the smaller details for later.

These arguments are just a few of the arguments for our faith. There are countless more, not to mention the evidence of what God has done in each of our lives and billions of other's. Maybe no single argument will be completely convincing but together these arguments form a comprehensive case for the coherence of our faith.

Book suggestion:

Tactics: A Game Plan for Discussing Your Christian Convictions by Greg Koukl.

---

[1] Ravi Zacharias, http://www.outreachmagazine.com/interviews/5623-ravi-zacharias-with-gentleness-and-respect.html/3

Learn This

1) Please write out the BEST FACTS and TALL TALES acronyms (see p. 114).

The BEST acronym (reasons to believe in God).
B - The **B**_____ of the universe points to God.
E - The **E**_____ of the universe points to God.
S - S_____ and morality point to God.
T - The **T**_____ about Jesus points to God.

The FACTS acronym (reasons to trust the Bible).
F - The Bible **F**_____ the future.
A - The Bible is **A**_____ accurate.
C - The Bible is **C**_____.
T - The Bible has been **T**_____ correctly.
S - The Bible is **S**_____ accurate.

The TALL acronym (reasons to reject other worldviews).
T - Other worldviews are **T**_____ incoherent.
A - Other worldviews make **A**_____ truth claims.
L - Other worldviews **L**_____ evidence and require a "leap of faith."
L - Other worldviews **L**_____ of power to change lives.

The TALES acronym (reasons to dismiss evolution).
T - The **T**_____ species are missing.
A - The **A**_____ of evolution is insufficient.
L - **L**_____ can't arise from non-life.
E - The **E**_____ of information and design is naturalistically inexplicable.
S - The **S**_____ of the universe from nothing is too.

2) How can you put what you learned in this lesson into practice when you deal with doubt?

3) How can you put what you learned in this lesson into practice when you defend your faith?

2
The Beginning of the Universe

B - The Beginning of the Universe Points to God.

Jesus claimed that God created the universe and everything in it (Mk. 10:6, 13:19). Scripture also claims that Jesus is creator God (Jn. 1:1-3, 14, Col. 1:16). It took science another two millennia to realize that the universe had to have a cause.

The beginning of the universe is the "B" in the BEST FACTS acronym. This argument has traditionally been called the cosmological argument for God's existence. Logic dictates and science corroborates a supernatural beginning of the universe out of nothing a finite time ago. Some might call it the "Big Bang" but we know it's what the Bible calls creation. The beginning of the universe points to God. This is the ultimate evidence for God's existence.

The value of logical arguments

If the premises of a logical argument cannot be refuted, the conclusion stands as a truth about reality. We'll refer to logical arguments for God's existence in this lesson and the next two. These arguments, if valid, are compelling evidence for God.

The Kalam cosmological argument (as stated by Dr. William Lane Craig):[1]

Premise 1: Everything that begins to exist has a cause of its existence.

Premise 2: The universe began to exist.

Conclusion: Therefore, the universe has a cause of its existence.

Over the years, this type of reasoning has convinced many intelligent people of God's existence. Einstein's work on Relativity convinced him that the universe had a beginning. Aware of the metaphysical implications of that, he tried to ignore his own findings, later calling it the biggest blunder of his career.[2] Although he never became a Christian, as far as we know, he did come to acknowledge the existence of a God, what he called, "a superior reasoning power, which is revealed in the incomprehensible universe…" and an "illimitable superior spirit who reveals himself in the slight details we are able to perceive."[3] The beginning of the universe is compelling evidence for God.

This argument is logically valid.

The atheist has trouble refuting the premises of the cosmological argument.

Premise 1: Everything that begins to exist has a cause of its existence.

To deny this, the atheist has to deny the law of causality. Most won't even try this. Some atheists try to trick people into believing that something can come from nothing. They usually do this by first defining nothing as something and then saying that "nothing" can produce something. Kind of crazy.

Skeptic Michael Shermer literally states that the "nothing of the vacuum of space" actually consists of space, time, energy, gravity, turbulence, and the laws of nature and then concludes that that "nothing" can produce "something."[4] Obviously, his nothing is really something and his trick might work on someone who is ignorantly unaware but not on anyone willing to consider real evidence.

Why do atheists try so hard to get something from nothing?

The bottom line, though, is that none of these atheists would deny the first law of thermodynamics, that tells us quite clearly that you can't get something from nothing.

Premise 2: The Universe began to exist.

There are only two real options to deny this. The cyclical model and the multiverse approach are the two ways people try to deny the second premise. The cyclical model has been refuted by modern science.[5] The multiverse model is not empirically testable and wouldn't refute God's existence even if it were true.

Since the atheist can't refute these premises, the atheist often tries to turn the tables, accusing us of appealing to a "God of the gaps." Unfortunately for them, we're not. We're believing what we know to be true of the universe, what is in alignment with science. They are appealing here to a science of the gaps. Since they can't refute these premises, the conclusion stands.

The universe had a supernatural beginning a finite time ago.

The redshift of light from distant galaxies, cosmic microwave background radiation, gravitational waves and other scientific data point to a beginning. That alone points to a self-existent, timeless, powerful, intelligent, and personal cause. These are the very attributes the Bible ascribes to God!

Why does the beginning of the universe point to God?

Agnostic Robert Jastrow, founding director of NASA's Goddard Institute for Space Studies, famously wrote, "For the scientist who has lived by his faith in the power of reason, the story ends like a bad dream. He has scaled the mountains of ignorance;

he is about to conquer the highest peak; as he pulls himself over the final rock he is greeted by a band of theologians who have been sitting there for centuries."

What does Jastrow, a renowned agnostic scientist, mean by this?

What about Entropy?

Entropy always increases across closed systems, like the universe, not necessarily in open ones, like the earth. That's why you shouldn't use the second law of thermodynamics to try to disprove evolution (there are better ways to do that). However, do use the second law to argue for the beginning of the universe. Since entropy has not reached infinity, we know the universe is not eternal!

Think of entropy like the E on your car's gas gauge. The longer you drive the closer you get to empty, or "E." As long as you're not on "E" you can be certain you haven't been driving forever; the gas (or order in the universe in this analogy) has to run out. Similarly, since we haven't reached total "E," or entropy, in the universe, we can know the universe has not been here forever either.

What about the Big Bang?

The "Big Bang" is a term renowned astronomer Fred Hoyle coined in derision as he sought to refute the scientific evidence for the beginning of the universe (atheism needs an eternal universe). The term stuck and the Big Bang has been the name scientists have used for the beginning of the universe ever since. The hostility towards this term among Christians is understandable. Many have heard the Big Bang offered as a rebuttal to creation. Fortunately, that rebuttal isn't justified. The beginning science has confirmed is great evidence for a Creator.

There is no legitimate naturalistic explanation for the cause of the universe. When you hear the term "Big Bang," realize that it is an admission of a beginning event. Atheists have no answer for how that could have happened without a Creator. Instead of fighting people on the term, use that as a point of common ground to begin discussing what could have caused the universe to exist. Ravi Zacharias does that by asking this great question: "If the Big Bang is where it all began … may I ask what preceded the Big Bang?"[7] You could ask something similar.

As Christians, we believe in creation, not a naturalistic origin of the universe. Use the Big Bang as a transition to the cosmological argument for God's existence. The scientific admission of the universe's beginning actually goes a long way towards proving our point and does devastating damage to atheism.

Activity: Your friend says, "I believe in the Big Bang." How do you bring this back to the evidence for God and the Gospel?

Conclusion

The cosmological argument for God's existence is convincing evidence for a self-existent, eternal, omnipotent, omniscient, omnipresent, omnibenevolent, intelligent, and personal Creator. This argument is logically valid and it is supported by the science as well. You can use this argument to demonstrate the existence of God and you can remind yourself of it when you face doubt. Believing in God is both rational and reasonable.

Book suggestion:

God's Crime Scene: A Cold-Case Detective Examines the Evidence for a Divinely Created Universe by J. Warner Wallace.

[1] William Lane Craig, The Kalam Cosmological Argument, p. 63. [2] Hugh Ross, The Creator and the Cosmos, p. 45. [3] Lincoln Barnett, The Universe and Dr. Einstein, Revised Edition, p. 109. [4] Michael Shermer, https://www.scientificamerican.com/article/much-ado-about-nothing/, [5] NASA, https://map.gsfc.nasa.gov/universe/uni_fate.html, [6] Robert Jastrow, God and the Astronomers (New and Expanded Edition), p. 107. [7] Ravi Zacharias, Jesus Among Other Gods: The Absolute Claims of the Christian Message, p. 64.

Learn This

1) Please write out the BEST FACTS and TALL TALES acronyms (see p. 114).

(see p. 114)

The BEST acronym (reasons to believe in God).
B - The **B**_____ of the universe points to God.
E - The **E**_____ of the universe points to God.
S - **S**_____ and morality point to God.
T - The **T**_____ about Jesus points to God.

The FACTS acronym (reasons to trust the Bible).
F - The Bible **F**_____ the future.
A - The Bible is **A**_____ accurate.
C - The Bible is **C**_____.
T - The Bible has been **T**_____ correctly.
S - The Bible is **S**_____ accurate.

The TALL acronym (reasons to reject other worldviews).
T - Other worldviews are **T**_____ incoherent.
A - Other worldviews make **A**_____ truth claims.
L - Other worldviews **L**_____ evidence and require a "leap of faith."
L - Other worldviews **L**_____ of power to change lives.

The TALES acronym (reasons to dismiss evolution).
T - The **T**_____ species are missing.
A - The **A**_____ of evolution is insufficient.
L - **L**_____ can't arise from non-life.
E - The **E**_____ of information and design is naturalistically inexplicable.
S - The **S**_____ of the universe from nothing is too.

2) How can you put what you learned in this lesson into practice when you deal with doubt?

3) How can you put what you learned in this lesson into practice when you defend your faith?

3
The Engineering of the Universe

E - The Engineering of the Universe Points to God.

Jesus claimed that the universe was created by God (Mk. 10:6, 13:19). He also taught that God was intimately involved in maintaining it (Matt. 6:25-30, Lk. 12:24-28). The engineering of universe points to God.

There are different types of design arguments. Most recognize the following facts. There are countless constants and parameters of the universe that must be exactly right for life to be possible on earth. Similarly, information is programmed into every component of the universe. This "fine-tuning" of the universe is evidence of an all powerful and good creator of life. This has been and continues to be a compelling argument for God's existence. The skeptic can't just ignore this.

The design argument (as stated by Dr. William Lane Craig):[1]

Premise 1: The universe is either the product of chance, necessity, or design.

Premise 2: The Universe is not the product of chance.

Premise 3: The Universe is not the product of necessity.

Conclusion: The Universe is the product of design.

 Over the years, this argument has convinced many intelligent people of God's existence. Before he died, Antony Flew, who was known as the world's most notorious atheist, came to believe in God's existence because of the design argument for God. He was particularly struck by the engineering apparent in biological systems.

This argument is logically valid.

To refute this argument the atheist must refute one of the premises.

Premise 1: The universe is either the product of chance, necessity, or design.

This is obvious and no one will try to refute it.

Premise 2: The Universe is not the product of chance.

To refute this, the atheist has to demonstrate the statistical probability of the universe, something that is ridiculously impossible.

Premise 3: The Universe is not the product of necessity.

To refute this, the atheist has to demonstrate natural laws that would have caused this universe, something they can't do. If they could, they'd have to give a natural cause for those laws and the universe itself, again, impossible.

Why does design best explain the engineering of the universe?

Because they can't refute the premises, the conclusion stands: The Universe is the product of design.

Intuitive appeal.

This argument is logically valid but it also hits on something that we know to be true. Design always implies a designer and most people know and accept this.

The Bible tells us this in Ps. 19:1-2, which states, "The heavens declare the glory of God; the skies proclaim the work of his hands. Day after day they pour forth speech;

night after night they display knowledge."

Many people know God exists simply by looking at His creation. In fact, the vast majority of people come to this conclusion. Famous philosophers like Alvin Plantinga and René Descartes have argued that belief in God is logically necessary.

How have you seen God in His creation?

Examples of design in the universe, our earth, and life.

The universe seems to be perfectly designed for life on earth and earth is uniquely situated in the universe. It is perfectly located in the only possible intersection of all nine habitable zones. These include the water habitable zone, the ultraviolet habitable zone, the photosynthetic habitable zone, the ozone habitable zone, the planetary rotation rate habitable zone, the planetary obliquity habitable zone, the tidal habitable zone, the stratosphere habitable zone, and the electric wind habitable zone.[2]

Numerous constants and parameters must be exactly perfect for life to be possible at all. A few examples of constants and parameters that must be perfect:

The distance between stars, the rate of luminosity increase for stars, the number of star companions, the gravitational interaction with a moon, the magnetic field, the axial tilt, the oxygen to nitrogen ratio in atmosphere, the carbon dioxide and water vapor levels in the atmosphere, the ozone level in the atmosphere, the atmospheric electric discharge rate, seismic activity, the ratio of electron to proton mass, the age of the universe, the entropy level of the universe, the mass of the universe, the stability of the proton, the fine structure constants, the velocity of light, the Beryllium-8, Carbon-12, and Oxygen-16 nuclear energy levels, and the weak nuclear force coupling constant.[3]

Examples of the statistics that imply design.

"If the neutron were not about 1.001 times the mass of the proton, all protons would have decayed into neutrons or all neutrons would have decayed into protons, and thus life would not be possible (Leslie, 1989, pp. 39-40)."[4]

"Calculations indicate that if the strong nuclear force, the force that binds protons and neutrons together in an atom, had been stronger or weaker by as little as 5%, life would be impossible (Leslie, 1989, pp. 4, 35; Barrow and Tipler, p. 322)."[4]

"If the electromagnetic force were slightly stronger or weaker, life would be impossible, for a variety of different reasons (Leslie, 1988, p. 299)."[4]

Life could not exist if the gravitational constant was off by 1 in 10^{60}.[1] There have not even been 10^{60} seconds since time began.

Life could not exist if the expansion rate was off by 1 in 10^{120}.[1]

The mass and energy of the early universe had to be evenly distributed to a precision of 1 in $10^{10^{123}}$.[1]

The problem of statistics applies to the origin of life as well. The simplest imaginable self-replicating cell would need about 100,000 nucleotide base pairs. Probability that 100,000 nucleotides and 10,000 amino acids would align in chiral order (using simple statistics 0.5x0.5 110,000 times = 0.5110,000 in base 10 = the following:) is 1 in $10^{33,113}$.[5] 1 in $10^{33,113}$ is the same as winning 4700 state lotteries in a row with only one ticket for each![5]

Probability of the components of the simplest imaginable organism aligning in order — 1 in $10^{112,827}$.[5] 1 in $10^{112,827}$ is the same as winning 16,119 state lotteries in a row with only one winning ticket.[5]

How do these statistics imply design in the universe?

The problem for the atheist.

Dembski has proposed a universal probability bound of 10^{-150}.[6] This means that anything outside of this would be literally statistically impossible.

In 2001, the odds that "any given planet in the universe would possess the necessary conditions to support intelligent physical life…shrank to less than one in a number so large it might as well be infinity (10^{173})."[7]

"The bottom line is that the universe is at least ten billion orders of magnitude (a factor of $10^{10,000,000,000}$ times) too small or too young for life to have assembled itself by natural processes."[3]

Because of these unfathomable statistics, many atheists and skeptics will naturally appeal to a hypothetical multiverse, claiming that in an infinite number of universes statistics would not matter. With that kind of logic Dawkins can naively appeal to luck[8] but that isn't a legitimate solution.

Other scientists are more honest. Physicist Paul Davies has a better answer: "There is for me powerful evidence that there is something going on behind it all…it seems as though somebody has fine-tuned nature's numbers to make the universe. The impression of design is overwhelming."[1] Astronomer Fred Hoyle agreed, "A common sense interpretation of the facts suggests that a super intellect has monkeyed with physics… and that there are no blind forces worth speaking about in nature. The numbers one calculates from the facts seem to me so overwhelming as to put this conclusion almost beyond question."[1]

What do you think of Davies and Hoyle's quotes?

The intelligent design movement.

The intelligent design movement has highlighted much of this. The science does seem to be building the case for an intelligent designer. Much of their research and many of their resources build a solid case for intelligent design.

The presence of design is obvious throughout the universe. This points many, whose minds are open to considering the evidence, to the conclusion that an intelligent designer exists.

Why do you think there has been such backlash against the Intelligent Design movement?

Conclusion

The design argument for God's existence is compelling and it is also intuitive. This makes it a particularly strong argument. Most people readily acknowledge that design implies a designer.

Bank on this when sharing and defending your faith. Feel free to frame the argument in a logical way, like described earlier. Use some of the statistics to demonstrate that if needed. Also be ready to apply to people's intuitions. Most people will already agree

Activity: Most people readily admit "something greater than ourselves out there." How could you help them find Jesus?

with this and may not even need an elaborate defense. When you're struggling with doubt, remind yourself that the universe really is too perfectly designed for it to be a product of chance.

Book suggestion:

On Guard: Defending your Faith with Reason and Precision by William Lane Craig.

[1] William Lane Craig, https://www.youtube.com/watch?v=qSa7cq3QOwU, [1] Hugh Ross, Improbable Planet: How Earth Became Humanity's Home. [2] Hugh Ross, http://www.reasons.org/articles/design-and-the-anthropic-principle. [3] Robin Collins, http://www.discovery.org/a/91 [5] Ralph Muncaster, Evolution Dismanteled, pp.138-142. [6] William Dembski, 1999. Intelligent Design, Chapter 6. Downers Grove, Illinois: IVP Academic. [7] Hugh Ross, http://www.reasons.org/articles/anthropic-principle-a-precise-plan-for-humanity. [8] Dawkins, The Selfish Gene (40th anniversary edition), p. 20.

Learn This

1) Please write out the BEST FACTS and TALL TALES acronyms (see p. 114).

The BEST acronym (reasons to believe in God).
B - The **B**_____ of the universe points to God.
E - The **E**_____ of the universe points to God.
S - **S**_____ and morality point to God.
T - The **T**_____ about Jesus points to God.

The FACTS acronym (reasons to trust the Bible).
F - The Bible **F**_____ the future.
A - The Bible is **A**_____ accurate.
C - The Bible is **C**_____.
T - The Bible has been **T**_____ correctly.
S - The Bible is **S**_____ accurate.

The TALL acronym (reasons to reject other worldviews).
T - Other worldviews are **T**_____ incoherent.
A - Other worldviews make **A**_____ truth claims.
L - Other worldviews **L**_____ evidence and require a "leap of faith."
L - Other worldviews **L**_____ of power to change lives.

The TALES acronym (reasons to dismiss evolution).
T - The **T**_____ species are missing.
A - The **A**_____ of evolution is insufficient.
L - **L**_____ can't arise from non-life.
E - The **E**_____ of information and design is naturalistically inexplicable.
S - The **S**_____ of the universe from nothing is too.

2) How can you put what you learned in this lesson into practice when you deal with doubt?

3) How can you put what you learned in this lesson into practice when you defend your faith?

4 Standards and Morality

S - Standards and Morality Point to God.

Jesus defined God as the standard of good (Mk. 10:18). Without a standard of good there would be no objective way of defining right and wrong. The objectivity of morality is compelling evidence for the existence of God.

This has traditionally been called the moral argument for God's existence. We all know some things are always right while others are always wrong. Objective morality can only exist if an objective moral law giver and enforcer (i.e. God) exists. If not, anything literally goes. We know anything doesn't go so we know God exists. If you believe in objective morality, justice and ethics, you agree God must exist.

The Moral argument (as stated by Dr. William Lane Craig):[1]

Premise 1: If God does not exist, objective moral values and duties do not exist.

Premise 2: Objective moral values and duties do exist.

Conclusion: Therefore, God exists.

Over the years, this argument has convinced many intelligent people of God's existence. These have included C. S. Lewis and world renowned scientist Francis Collins (who led the human genome project and is now director of the National Institutes of Health).

Clearing up some confusion.

This argument is not meant to imply that atheists can't be moral or ethical. It simply clarifies that if God does not exist there is no such thing as objective morality.

Additionally, this argument does not define what is moral. That is beyond its scope. It simply

Why isn't just being good good enough?

demonstrates that if anything is objectively right or wrong, God must exist. As Christians, we believe the Bible gives us a framework for knowing what is right and wrong. The FACTS acronym will demonstrate some of the reasons we can trust the Bible and what it says about morality.

This argument is logically valid.

To refute the moral argument, atheists must refute one of its two premises.

Premise 1: If God does not exist, objective moral values and duties do not exist.

Most atheists will assume this.

Dawkins wrote, "In a universe of electrons and selfish genes, blind physical forces and genetic replication, some people are going to get hurt, other people are going to get lucky, and you won't find any rhyme or reason in it, nor any justice. The universe that we observe has precisely the properties we should expect if there is, at bottom, no design, no purpose, no evil, no good, nothing but pitiless indifference."[2]

What is Dawkins admitting about morality and God in this quote?

Most people recognize the insanity of this. Torturing babies, raping innocent women, and mass genocide are actually wrong and ought not be done. The atheist can refute this but at a very steep cost; they have to give up all objective ethical standards.

Premise 2: objective moral values and duties do exist.
Some intelligent atheists recognize the insanity of denying premise one and try to attack premise two. They might appeal to a brute fact theory. Intelligently, they'd never allow that kind of argument for anything else (like God's existence). This argument is unsupportable.

Since the atheist can't really get out of the premises, the truth that God exists stands.

People naturally know there is an objective moral law.

C. S. Lewis articulated this well stating, "My argument against God was that the universe seemed so cruel and unjust. Just how had I got this idea of just and unjust? A man does not call a line crooked unless he has some idea of a straight line. What was I comparing this universe with when I called it unjust? … Thus in the very act of trying to prove that God did not exist—in other words, that the whole of reality was senseless—I found I was forced to assume that one part of reality—namely my idea of justice—was full of sense. Consequently atheism turns out to be too simple.

If the whole universe has no meaning, we should never have found out that it has no meaning."[3]

Even though different societies disagree on some aspects of morality, they don't disagree on the fundamentals; they simply define terms differently. Everyone knows murder, rape, and stealing are wrong; some just define those terms differently than others.

Just like ignorance of math is not a valid argument against math, this is no valid rebuttal of the moral law.

What are some moral absolutes there is near universal agreement on?

Different views on ethics and morality.

Subjective views are ones that derive from the subject. The following eight are examples of this.

logic determines morality (Kant's Categorical Imperative). Depending on your foundational assumptions, you'll get very different conclusions.

Utilitarianism. The greatest good is what is best. Who decides what is the greatest good makes this helplessly subjective.

Evolutionary morality. In spite of falling to the genetic fallacy, this approach, if true, would only explain why we feel certain ways, it would not prescribe how we ought to act.

Social contract theory. This view is inherently flawed as it would justify Hitler's holocaust and many other genocides and atrocities that were socially accepted.

Rights-based morality. It is difficult to affirm the existence of rights except by appealing to God or societal laws. Obviously an appeal to societal laws would be subjective while an appeal to rights ordained by God would simply be an appeal to divine laws (something we'll consider shortly).
Ethical egoism. Doing what is in one's own best interest is inherently subjective.

Virtue ethics. This ancient approach would fail to justify why one ought or ought not behave in certain ways.

Moral subjectivism. This is inherently subjective.

Objective views are ones that derive from outside of the subjects but to which subjects are accountable. The following two are examples of this.

Brute fact theory. This assumes objective moral values and duties but fails to define them or explain where they could derive from.

Divine command theory. This is the only approach that gives an objective description of morality. Which moral commands are accepted should depend on the validity and coherence of the worldview in question. God is the only coherent explanation for objective moral values and duties.

How does God provide an objective basis for morality?

Make your examples clear.

When using this argument, use extreme examples, and ones that are socially relevant. You might ask if the atheist believes Hitler's holocaust, torturing babies or gay-bashing are morally justifiable. Of course, they'd never agree to this. If they do, they're betraying their bias.

Also make sure to appeal to peoples' intuition. They know certain things are right and certain things are wrong. They know they ought not hate and ought to love. These strong convictions point to the existence of God.

How this relates to the problem of pain.

Epicurus (~300 BC) articulated the 'the Epicurean paradox,' stating, "God either wishes to take away evils, and is unable; or He is able and unwilling; or He is neither willing nor able; or He is both willing and able."[4] Of course, if either of the first three options were true, God would not really be God and if the last were true, there should be no evil. This formulation of the problem of pain and evil is a powerful objection to our faith.

There are good answers to that but first, the atheist that gives this rebuttal must realize he is assuming a standard of right and wrong by which evil is defined. Dr. Frank Turek explains how the atheist has to steal from God to make his point against God.[5] In other words, to make this accusation, the atheist must assume an objective moral standard, something that requires the existence of God.

As Christians, we know evil exists, that it isn't created by God but it is the failure to measure up to God and His objective standard of right and wrong. We also have a hope that in spite of the evil that free human beings cause, our sovereign God can bring good out of it (Rom. 8:28).

> *Activity: How would you answer a friend who claimed that the existence of evil disproves God?*

Conclusion

Everyone intuitively believes that certain behaviors are right and others are wrong. No one would permit you to steal their wallet if you claimed you thought it was OK. People everywhere recognize evil when they see it. The moral argument for God's existence takes that common knowledge and helps people recognize that if objective morality exists, God must also.

When sharing and defending your faith, ask lots of questions and use clear examples that will demonstrate the reality of this argument. Also be encouraged, world class intellectuals have come to Christ through this argument. When dealing with doubt, remember to remind yourself of the truth that standards and morality point to the existence of God.

Book suggestion:

Stealing from God: Why Atheists Need God to Make Their Case by Frank Turek.

[1] William Lane Craig, Reasonable Faith: Christian Truth and Apologetics, p.172. [2] Richard Dawkins, River Out of Eden: A Darwinian View of Life. [3] C.S. Lewis, Mere Christianity, pp. 45–46. [4] Douglas Groothuis, Christian Apologetics, p.616, [5] Frank Turek, Stealing from God: Why Atheists Need God to Make Their Case.

Learn This

1) Please write out the BEST FACTS and TALL TALES acronyms (see p. 114).

The BEST acronym (reasons to believe in God).
B - The **B**_____ of the universe points to God.
E - The **E**_____ of the universe points to God.
S - **S**_____ and morality point to God.
T - The **T**_____ about Jesus points to God.

The FACTS acronym (reasons to trust the Bible).
F - The Bible **F**_____ the future.
A - The Bible is **A**_____ accurate.
C - The Bible is **C**_____.
T - The Bible has been **T**_____ correctly.
S - The Bible is **S**_____ accurate.

The TALL acronym (reasons to reject other worldviews).
T - Other worldviews are **T**_____ incoherent.
A - Other worldviews make **A**_____ truth claims.
L - Other worldviews **L**_____ evidence and require a "leap of faith."
L - Other worldviews **L**_____ of power to change lives.

The TALES acronym (reasons to dismiss evolution).
T - The **T**_____ species are missing.
A - The **A**_____ of evolution is insufficient.
L - **L**_____ can't arise from non-life.
E - The **E**_____ of information and design is naturalistically inexplicable.
S - The **S**_____ of the universe from nothing is too.

2) How can you put what you learned in this lesson into practice when you deal with doubt?

3) How can you put what you learned in this lesson into practice when you defend your faith?

5
The Truth About Jesus

T - The Truth About Jesus Points to God.

Jesus demonstrated the Bible's claim that He was God in human flesh through His miraculous life, death, and resurrection. He foretold his resurrection and His resurrection is the foundation of our faith (Matt. 16:21, Jn. 2:18-22, 1 Cor. 15:17).

The gospel accounts are trustworthy and historical. The evidence for Jesus' life, death and resurrection is overwhelming. The evidence for the resurrection is particularly irrefutable. You should commit this evidence to memory and use it often. As C.S. Lewis states, Jesus was either a liar, lunatic or Lord and God. The evidence supports the latter! We can trust Him and the Bible He affirmed. That leads us to the validity of scripture. Here is some of the evidence for Jesus and his resurrection.

There is a wealth of evidence for Jesus.

Historical evidence corroborates Jesus' life, ministry, death, and resurrection. There are as many non-Christian historical references to Jesus as to Tiberias Caesar. Including Christian references, there are four times as many historical references.[1]

Here are some Extra-biblical sources quoted by J. Warner Wallace:[2]

Phlegon - Pronounced Flegon - (80-140AD), also mentioned by Julius Africanus, wrote a chronicle of history around 140AD: Jesus had the ability to accurately predict the future, was crucified under the reign of Tiberius and demonstrated His wounds after he was resurrected.

Thallus (52AD) quoted by Julius Africanus, writing around 221AD: There was an earthquake and darkness at the point of Jesus' crucifixion.

Tacitus - Pronounced Tasitus - (56-120AD) was a senator under Emperor Vespasian and proconsul of Asia: Jesus lived in Judea, was crucified under Pontius Pilate, and his followers were persecuted for their faith.

Mara Bar-Serapion (70AD): Jesus was a wise and influential man who died for His beliefs. The Jewish leadership was responsible for His death. Jesus' followers adopted His beliefs and lived their lives accordingly.

Pliny the Younger - Pronounced plin(as in sin)-y - (61-113AD), in a letter to the Roman emperor Trajan: the first Christians believed Jesus was God, the first Christians upheld a high moral code, and these early followers met regularly to worship Jesus.

Suetonius - Pronounced Sootonious - (69-140AD), a Roman historian and annalist of the Imperial House under the Emperor Hadrian: They were committed to their belief Jesus was God and withstood the torment and punishment of the Roman Empire. Jesus had a curious and immediate impact on His followers, empowering them to die courageously for what they knew was true.

Lucian - Pronounced Looseean - of Samosata: (115-200 A.D.), a Greek satirist: Jesus taught about repentance and about the family of God. These teachings were quickly adopted by Jesus' followers and exhibited to the world around them.

Celsus - Pronounced Sellsus - (175AD): Jesus had an earthly father who was a carpenter, possessed magical powers and claimed to be God.

Josephus (37-101AD) a first century historian: Jesus lived in Palestine, was a wise man and a teacher, worked amazing deeds, was accused by the Jews, crucified under Pilate and had followers called Christians.

What do you think of these extra-biblical references to christ?

There is a wealth of evidence for Jesus' resurrection.

The testimony of the resurrection occurred very early. It is not a myth that evolved. There were hundreds of eyewitnesses who saw the risen Christ. Jesus' tomb was found empty three days after He was buried. There are no historical denials of the empty tomb. The criteria of embarrassment (like women finding the risen Lord, the disciples' doubt, etc.) demonstrate historicity. Even hostile rebuttals admitted the empty tomb and key elements of the resurrection. The Babylonian Talmud claims that Jesus was raised through incantation and states, "woe to him who makes himself alive by the name of God."[3]

John described pericardial effusion (Jn. 19:34), a scientific and medical reality that also demonstrated he was an eyewitness. Some claim that divergent accounts hurt the case for the resurrection. They are wrong. Divergent accounts are not truly contradictory and actually demonstrate eyewitness credibility. The disciples adamantly claimed a falsifiable bodily resurrection. This would have been easy to disprove. Millenia after the fact, the bodily resurrection still cannot be refuted.

The historical evidence for the resurrection is compelling and alternative theories fail to convince. Gary Habermas struggled with doubt earlier in life but became convinced by the evidence for the resurrection. He is the authority on the resurrection and has defended it around the world. Next we'll look at his minimal facts approach.

Habermas' Minimal Facts.

There is nearly universal scholarly agreement on the following twelve facts.[4] Habermas and Licona have also used a shortened version of this list, defending the resurrection with only points 1, 4, 5, 11, and 12.[5] Whether you use all twelve facts or the abbreviated five, these facts confirm the historical truth of the resurrection.

1. Jesus died by Roman crucifixion.
2. He was buried in a private tomb.
3. His disciples were initially discouraged.
4. Jesus' tomb was found empty shortly after His burial.
5. The disciples and numerous others were convinced they saw the risen Christ.
6. Their lives were completely transformed - even to the point of being willing to be persecuted and martyred.
7. The story of the resurrection took place very early - at the beginning of church history.
8. Their testimony and preaching took place initially in Jerusalem. This is the one place the resurrection could have been refuted.
9. Based on the the gospel and the message of the resurrection, the church grew.
10. Sunday became the primary day for gathering and worshipping. Jewish believers switched from the Sabbath to Sunday over it.
11. James, the brother of Jesus, went from skeptic to believer because of seeing the risen Christ.
12. Saul, a persecutor of Christians, did too and later became the Apostle Paul.

Activity: Consider the minimal facts, the historical method, and the resurrection hypotheses. Then consider which theory explains more of the minimal facts most convincingly. Check the box for the theory that you think wins.

The Historical Method[6]

1. Explanatory scope - Hypothesis explains more of the data than other hypotheses.

2. Explanatory power - Hypothesis best explains the data.

3. Plausibility - Hypothesis is implied by more of the data than other theories are.

4. Less ad hoc - Hypothesis does not string together unwarranted hypotheses.

5. Hypothesis is disconfirmed by fewer accepted beliefs than other Hypotheses are.

6. Hypothesis surpasses other hypotheses in points 1 and 5 such that other hypotheses have little chance of surpassing it.

Resurrection Hypotheses

☐ Resurrection is a myth that evolved.

☐ Resurrection was just plagiarized from pagan myths.

☐ Judas magically died in Jesus' place (the Islamic response).

☐ The body was moved.

☐ The body was stolen.

☐ Swoon theory (Jesus resuscitated in the tomb and escaped).

☐ Jesus had a twin brother.

☐ Jesus was never buried.

☐ Eyewitness accounts were just mass hallucinations.

☐ Resurrections don't happen.

☐ Jesus physically rose from the dead.

The best explanation for the data.

The only theory that satisfies the data is a resurrection. The only true rebuttal is a presupposition of metaphysical naturalism. Of course, this is a logical fallacy and it even falls prey to these data.

This is a powerful argument that even the brightest critics cannot refute without appealing to their own presuppositions. Ehrman gives a ridiculous rebuttal to the evidence for the resurrection but then admits, "Am I proposing that this is what really happened? Absolutely not! …From a purely historical point of view, a highly unlikely event is far more probable than a virtually impossible one."[6] Here he is using a logical fallacy, called begging the question, to refute the resurrection. He is appealing to metaphysical naturalism, his own presupposition, to make his case.

> *What do weak skeptical rebuttals tell you about the strength of the evidence for the resurrection?*

If the data confirm that a resurrection happened, the presupposition of metaphysical naturalism is no longer tenable. Miracles can happen. The supernatural cannot be written off. Skeptics often state that supernatural claims cannot be considered but the evidence for the resurrection dismantles their attack. For a broader rebuttal of metaphysical naturalism, check out Craig Keener's book *Miracles*.

Why this matters.

Paul told believers, in 1 Corinthians 15:17, "if Christ has not been raised, your faith is futile…" Only Christianity has a Savior that demonstrated power over death. Who else could you reasonably trust your eternity to? The one event that is most unique and foundational to our faith happens to be the one event most attested by the evidence.

Why should Jesus and the resurrection be the focus of our apologetics?

Conclusion

Jesus is God. The Bible claims this directly (ex. Matt. 1:23, Jn. 1:1, 20:28, Acts 20:28, etc.), prophetically (ex. Zech. 11:12-13, 12:10, etc.), textually (ex. the NT authors used the Greek word for Lord, κύριος, pronounced kurios, for YHWH but also for Jesus hundreds of times, etc.), and practically (ex. Is. 45:23 & Php. 2:10-11, etc.). Jesus also claimed this of himself directly (ex. Jn. 5:18 and 8:58, etc.) and practically (ex. Mk. 2:10, 28, etc.). The church has believed this since its inception. Just like height, length, and width make up one essence, three dimensional space, so too God exists as three in one. Jesus is fully God.

Some critics argue that Jesus was just an apocalyptic prophet whose followers morphed him into a deity. Ehrman is famous for such criticisms. Michael Bird, Craig Evans, Simon Gathercole, Charles E. Hill, and Chris Tilling obliterate that argument in their book *How God Became Jesus: The Real Origins of Belief in Jesus' Divine Nature.*

Jesus' life, ministry, death, and resurrection showed He was truly God. The resurrection is great evidence for God and for the reliability of the Christian faith. Confidently communicate the evidence for the resurrection when you share and defend your faith. Make sure to remind yourself of this when you face doubt. Jesus conquered death and that changes everything!

Book suggestion:

The Case for the Resurrection of Jesus by Gary Habermas and Mike Licona.

[1] Ryan Turner, https://carm.org/jesus-exist, [2] J. Warner Wallace, http://coldcasechristianity.com/2014/is-there-any-evidence-for-jesus-outside-the-bible/, [3] The Cradle the Cross and the Crown, [4] Gary Habermas, The Historical Jesus: Ancient Evidence for the Life of Christ, p. 158, [5] Gary Habermas and Mike Licona, The Case for the Resurrection of Jesus, pp. 48-69, [6] Christopher Behan McCullagh, Justifying Historical Descriptions (Cambridge Studies in Philosophy), p. 19, [7] Bart Ehrman, Jesus, Interrupted: Revealing the Hidden Contradictions in the Bible (And Why We Don't Know About Them), p.177.

Learn This

1) Please write out the BEST FACTS and TALL TALES acronyms (see p. 114).

The BEST acronym (reasons to believe in God).
B - The **B**_____ of the universe points to God.
E - The **E**_____ of the universe points to God.
S - **S**_____ and morality point to God.
T - The **T**_____ about Jesus points to God.

The FACTS acronym (reasons to trust the Bible).
F - The Bible **F**_____ the future.
A - The Bible is **A**_____ accurate.
C - The Bible is **C**_____.
T - The Bible has been **T**_____ correctly.
S - The Bible is **S**_____ accurate.

The TALL acronym (reasons to reject other worldviews).
T - Other worldviews are **T**_____ incoherent.
A - Other worldviews make **A**_____ truth claims.
L - Other worldviews **L**_____ evidence and require a "leap of faith."
L - Other worldviews **L**_____ of power to change lives.

The TALES acronym (reasons to dismiss evolution).
T - The **T**_____ species are missing.
A - The **A**_____ of evolution is insufficient.
L - **L**_____ can't arise from non-life.
E - The **E**_____ of information and design is naturalistically inexplicable.
S - The **S**_____ of the universe from nothing is too.

2) How can you put what you learned in this lesson into practice when you deal with doubt?

3) How can you put what you learned in this lesson into practice when you defend your faith?

6
The Bible Foretells the Future

F - The Bible Foretells the Future.

Jesus claimed that the Bible was prophetic and clearly demonstrated how Old Testament prophecies about the Messiah applied to Him (Matt. 26:56).

Several hundred Biblical prophecies have been accurately fulfilled with more being fulfilled in modern times. This is conclusive evidence of God's fingerprints on scripture. Jesus alone fulfilled more than 100 prophecies. This can't be explained away.

Some might claim these prophecies are ambiguous and irrelevant. They are wrong. Although some prophecies are undoubtedly vague, many are convincingly strong.

Why prophecy matters

Prophecy is evidence of divine revelation. God's Word demonstrates its superiority over all other religious texts in this. Prophecy is also important in that it destroys the presupposition of metaphysical naturalism. If prophecy can accurately predict future events, the naturalistic view of the universe is untenable.

Alexander the Great is an example of someone who was convinced of prophecy in the Bible. In the Antiquities of the Jews 11.337, Josephus wrote, "And when the Book of Daniel was showed him wherein Daniel declared that one of the Greeks should destroy the empire of the Persians, he supposed that himself was the person intended."

Although critics try to write this off as a later fabrication, they are stuck with evidences for the veracity of Josephus' claim. The Samaritans were allowed to keep their temple, Alexander didn't give the Jews any new privileges, and Alexander's vision of the God of the Jews are all features that a fabrication would have avoided.[1]

A few examples of biblical prophecy.

Daniel 8 includes a prophecy of Alexander the Great. This is the prophecy Alexander the Great noticed of himself when he read it in Jerusalem. It predicted that the first king of Greece would conquer the dual kingdom of the Medo-Persians. It also stated that the first king of Greece would die at a young age, not by human cause, and that his kingdom would be split into four weaker kingdoms, that would then give rise to one that would persecute God's people.

All of this happened exactly as foretold. The critic's only response is that it was written after the fact, although that argument falls apart.[2] The fact that history records that Alexander read the prophecy of himself is one of the reasons we know it predates him.

Daniel 2:37-42 predicted the kingdoms that would rule for the next 500 years. This prophecy accurately predicted the kingdoms of Babylon, Medo-Persia, Greece, and Rome.[3]

Isaiah 44:28-45:7 includes an unbelievable prophecy of Cyrus the Great (Cyrus II of Persia). This prophecy mentioned Cyrus by name about 150 years before he was even born. It also predicted many details of his life (like the fact that he would subdue nations and mandate that Jerusalem be rebuilt).[4] As with Daniel, critics have tried to argue that this was all written after the fact but evidence confirms that is not the case.[3]

Amos 9:14-15 predicted Israel's rebirth as a nation. Is. 66:8 prophesied Israel's rebirth in a day, which happened on May 14, 1948. Hosea 11:11 prophesied that God's people would return to Israel via the air (prophetic of modern transportation). Jer. 31:23 and Zeph. 3:9 prophesied the rebirth of the Hebrew language. The history of Israel is unparalleled in human history. never has a nation displaced for millennia returned to their homeland in the way that Israel has. The facts that this was prophesied in scripture makes it that much more amazing.

Some have even claimed that Ezekiel prophesied the year of Israel's return and re-birth as a nation in 1948.[5] Ezekiel chapter 4 prophesies 430 years of exile for God's people. The first 70 of those were the Babylonian exile prophesied in Jer. 25. That left 360 years of exile for Israel according to Ezekiel's prophecy. Chuck Missler notes that Israel did not repent and according to Lev. 26:18, their punishment was multiplied 7 times resulting in 2,520 Hebrew calendar years (360 days per year) or 2,483 solar years. This is the number of years between the end of the Babylonian captivity and Israel's rebirth in 1948.[5]

How the skeptics circumvent biblical prophecy.

Most skeptics will split up books and charge that they were authored historically after the fact rather than prophetically before the events described. They don't do this because of the evidence, they do this because of their presupposition of metaphysical naturalism and their belief that prophecy is not possible. Modern scholarship continues to demonstrate that their rebuttals are unfounded.[3, 4]

Why are skeptics so committed to refuting biblical prophecy?

These are just a few examples of biblical prophecy. There are many others. These illustrate the prophetic nature of the Bible. In addition to hundreds of biblical prophecies, the Bible is full of many Messianic prophecies about Jesus.

We've tried to stress the importance of keeping apologetics focused on Jesus. You can do that by highlighting the Messianic prophecies about Him. The Messianic prophecies are also the hardest ones for skeptics to refute making these an important focus of apologetics.

8 Messianic prophecies that Jesus fulfilled.

Jesus fulfilled more than 100 prophecies (some would say that He fulfilled more than 300). The chance of 1 person fulfilling just 8 of these has been calculated at 1 in 10^{17}.[6] This demonstrates the impossibility of these prophecies being fulfilled by chance. Remember, Jesus fulfilled more than 100, so these prophecies truly demonstrate both the prophetic nature of the Bible and the significance of Jesus Christ.

The Messianic prophecies are also unique in that there are manuscripts containing these OT prophecies that predate Christ. In other words, the critic cannot claim that these were written after the fact. Let's look at 8 of these Messianic prophecies.

1) **2 Sam. 7:12-16, Jer. 23:5, Ps. 89:3-4 all predicted that Jesus would be a descendant of David.** Matthew 1:1, 6 and Luke 3:31 confirm Jesus' genealogy and the fact that he was a descendant of David.

2) **Daniel 9:24-27 prophesied the exact time of Jesus' arrival.** Josh McDowell describes this prophecy in fascinating detail.[7] Artaxerxes decreed the rebuilding of Jerusalem in 444 BC (Neh. 2:1-8) beginning the seventy seven's of Daniel's prophecy. The first sixty-nine seven's totaled 483 Hebrew calendar years) from the decree till the Messiah. 483 Hebrew calendar years are equal to 173,880 days, since the Hebrew calendar year was a 360 day year. Daniel's 483 Hebrew calendar years are equivalent to 476 solar years. Starting with 444 BC, when Artaxerxes decreed the rebuilding of Jerusalem, and adding 476 years, according to Daniel's prophecy, results in a date of 33 AD for the Messiah's entry into Jerusalem to be put to death in order to atone for our sin. This was all fulfilled (Mt. 21:1-11, John 12:12-16).

3) **Isaiah 7:14 foretold Jesus' virgin Birth.** Luke 1:26-38 explains the fulfillment of this prophecy. The possibility of a virgin birth is something that we accept by faith. Where he can be tested, Luke, the author of both Luke and Acts, proves to be an incredibly accurate historian.[8] His reporting of this miracle should not be questioned simply because of a presupposition of naturalism.

4) **Micah 5:1-2 prophesied that Jesus would be born in Bethlehem.** Matthew 2, Luke 2, and John 7:42 describe the fulfillment of this prophecy.

5) Isaiah 40:3 and Malachi 3:1 predicted that Jesus would be preceded by John the Baptist. Matthew 3, 11, Mark 1, Luke 7, and John 1 and 3 describe the fulfillment of this.

6) Isaiah 35:5-6 prophesied that Jesus would do miracles. The Gospels record numerous miracles that Jesus performed. Extra-biblical sources, like Phlegon, Celsus, Josephus, and the Babylonian Talmud, corroborate Jesus' supernatural powers (sometimes from critical perspectives). As with the virgin birth, the critic must appeal to a presupposition of metaphysical naturalism to deny these.

7) Psalm 22:16, Isaiah 53, and Zechariah 12:10 foretold Jesus' death by crucifixion. Jesus' crucifixion is recorded in the Gospels. It is also a fact of history. [8,9] Crucifixion began being practiced in the 6th century BCE.[10] David wrote Psalm 22 in the eleventh century BCE.[11] Isaiah was written in the 8th century BCE.[3] Zechariah was written in the sixth century BCE.[3] In other words, these passages spoke prophetically of Jesus' crucifixion but they were also likely prophetic of crucifixion itself.

8) Psalm 16:10, Isaiah 53:10-11, and John 2:18-22 predicted Jesus' resurrection from the dead. In addition to prophesying Jesus' crucifixion, scripture prophetically foretold Christ's resurrection as well (Psalm 16:10 and Isaiah 53:10-11). Jesus even prophesied his own resurrection as well (John 2:18-22). Jesus' resurrection is also a fact of history that believers can be confident in[8,9] (remember what we learned in chapter five).

Again, these are just 8 Messianic prophecies out of more than a hundred. Not only is the Bible prophetically accurate, it prophetically points to Jesus, the cornerstone of the Christian faith. These Messianic prophecies highlight the trustworthiness of scripture and the person and ministry of Jesus, our Savior.

What is so significant about these Messianic prophecies?

Conclusion

The prophetic nature of scripture demonstrates God's fingerprints on His word. There is no other religious text that comes anywhere near the prophetic reliability of the Bible. Hundreds of biblical prophecies have already been fulfilled and more are in our lifetime as well. The Bible is trustworthy.

Critics try to circumvent these prophecies by appealing to metaphysical naturalism, something that is not justified. The biblical and historical support for these prophecies, especially the Messianic ones, is incredible evidence for the Divine inspiration of God's word. Critics will often try to refute other prophecies they believe were false. There are great answers for each of their criticisms.

This is not the only argument for our faith but it is one more piece in the comprehensive case for it. It is also one that can be helpful in apologetical conversations. Also remember to remind yourself of these truths when you find yourself doubting God's word.

Book suggestion:

Evidence That Demands a Verdict: Life-Changing Truth for a Skeptical World by Josh McDowell and Sean McDowell.

[1] Alexander the Great visits Jerusalem, http://www.livius.org/sources/content/josephus/jewish-antiquities/alexander-the-great-visits-jerusalem/, [2] Wayne Jackson, https://www.christiancourier.com/articles/869-amazing-prophecy-in-the-book-of-daniel-an, [3] Merrill, Rooker, and Grisanti, The World and the Word: An Introduction to the Old Testament, [4] Norm Geisler, The Baker Encyclopedia of Christian Apologetics, p. 613. [5] Chuck Missler, http://www.khouse.org/articles/2000/276/, [6] Josh McDowell, The New Evidence that Demands a Verdict, p. 194, [7] Josh McDowell, The New Evidence that Demands a Verdict, p. 197-201. [8] Craig Keener, Acts: An Exegetical Commentary: Introduction and 1:1-2:47, p. 220. [8] Gary Habermas, The Historical Jesus: Ancient Evidence for the Life of Christ, p. 158, [9] Gary Habermas and Mike Licona, The Case for the Resurrection of Jesus, pp. 48-69, [10] Retief and Cilliers, The history and pathology of crucifixion, S Air Med J., 2003. [11] https://www.blueletterbible.org/study/parallel/paral18.cfm.

Learn This

1) Please write out the BEST FACTS and TALL TALES acronyms (see p. 114).

The BEST acronym (reasons to believe in God).
B - The **B**_____ of the universe points to God.
E - The **E**_____ of the universe points to God.
S - **S**_____ and morality point to God.
T - The **T**_____ about Jesus points to God.

The FACTS acronym (reasons to trust the Bible).
F - The Bible **F**_____ the future.
A - The Bible is **A**_____ accurate.
C - The Bible is **C**_____.
T - The Bible has been **T**_____ correctly.
S - The Bible is **S**_____ accurate.

The TALL acronym (reasons to reject other worldviews).
T - Other worldviews are **T**_____ incoherent.
A - Other worldviews make **A**_____ truth claims.
L - Other worldviews **L**_____ evidence and require a "leap of faith."
L - Other worldviews **L**_____ of power to change lives.

The TALES acronym (reasons to dismiss evolution).
T - The **T**_____ species are missing.
A - The **A**_____ of evolution is insufficient.
L - **L**_____ can't arise from non-life.
E - The **E**_____ of information and design is naturalistically inexplicable.
S - The **S**_____ of the universe from nothing is too.

2) How can you put what you learned in this lesson into practice when you deal with doubt?

3) How can you put what you learned in this lesson into practice when you defend your faith?

7
The Bible is Archeologically Accurate

A - The Bible is <u>A</u>rcheologically Accurate.

Jesus often described people, places, and events from the Old Testament as accurate history (a few examples include Matt. 8:11, 10:15,12:39-40, 24:15, 37-39, Lk. 11:51, 17:28-32, Jn. 3:14, 6:31, and 8:56-58). Jesus affirmed that the Bible was historically accurate. Archeology continues to confirm that claim.

It has been said that no archeological find has ever disproved the Bible.[1] The Bible is historically accurate as God's Word must be. Many archeological finds continue to affirm the trustworthiness of the Bible. The Bible's accurate history requires that it be treated with respect.

Archeological reliability.

The Bible is archeologically reliable. You can still visit many of the places and things the Bible talks about. Additionally, archeological findings continue to demonstrate the historical reliability of the Bible.

Why does archeology matter?

What about things there isn't much evidence for?

Remember, "Absence of evidence isn't evidence of absence." History has confirmed the reliability of the Bible again and again (there are countless examples of people groups, locations, and events that critics). More finds are happening all of the time. For example, the biblical city of Sodom was recently found!

Archeology confirms the reliability of the Bible.

There are so many fascinating examples of this. We'll look at just a few.

Lawrence Mykytiuk, of Purdue University, highlights the following people listed in the Old Testament who have been confirmed by archeology.[2] These include Shishak, So, Tirhakah, Necho II, Hophra, Mesha, Hadadezer, Ben-hadad, son of Hadadezer, Hazael, Ben-hadad, son of Hazael, Rezin, Omri, Ahab, Jehu, Joash, Jeroboam II, Menahem, Pekah, Hoshea, Sanballat "I," King David, Uzziah (Azariah), Ahaz, Hezekiah, Manasseh, Hilkiah, Shaphan, Azariah, Gemariah, Jehoiachin, Shelemiah,

Jehucal, Pashhur, Gedaliah, Tiglath-pileser III, Shalmaneser V, Sargon II, Sennacherib, Adrammelech, Esarhaddon, Merodach-baladan II, Nebuchadnezzar II, Nebo-sarsekim, Evil-merodach, Belshazzar, son and co-regent of Nabonidus, Cyrus the Great, Darius the Great, Xerxes I, Artaxerxes I, and Darius II. These are just a few and there are others.

The Temple Mount Sifting Project has found bullae mentioning nineteen biblical cities. These include Eltolad, Lachish, Nezib, Arab, Keilah, Gebim, Maon, Jagur, Gath, Bethul, Aphekah, Gibeah, Adullam, Zaanannaim, Socoh, Gibeon, Zarah, Adoraim, and Ziph. These are just a few cities confirmed by archeology. There are many more, including ones you can visit today.[3]

There are numerous other examples. The historical reliability of Acts is another famous one. Dr. Craig Keener has recently published the longest commentary on any biblical book in history on the book of Acts. He has demonstrated numerous historical parallels between Acts and first century evidence from the area.[4] Another scholar, Dr. Richard Bauckham, has demonstrated many eyewitness features in the Gospels.[5] Dr. Steven Collins has led the Tall el-Hammam Excavation Project, which he has recently associated with the biblical city of Sodom.[6]

These are just a few examples of some of the archeology that confirms the reliability of the Bible. Next we'll look at a few more examples of specific archeological finds that do the same.

How does this evidence encourage you?

A few examples

The Merneptah Stele: The earliest reference to Israel in the ancient world. It confirms Israel's presence and timeframe in Canaan.

The Dead Sea Scrolls: Found in the 1940s and demonstrated the textual integrity of the OT. A new cave was just found and more scrolls may be soon as well.

The Moabite Stone: Also confirms Israel's place in the ancient world and its interactions with Moab.

The Tel Dan Inscription: The first evidence of King David. There is more now as well.

The Ketef Hinnom Amulet Scrolls: Include God's name YHWH and phrases from various OT books including Num. 6:24-26. It's from the 4th century BCE and supports the validity of the OT.

Baruch's Bulla: Jeremiah's scribe's bullae are debated.

Ahimaaz's Bulla: Ahimaaz was one of Solomon's deputies.

Hezekiah's Bulla: This bulla is the biblical King Hezekiah's seal.

Jezebel's Seal: Archeologists have found the seal of King Ahab's evil queen.

King Uzziah's Burial Plaque: It indicates Uzziah's possible burial place.

House of Yahweh Ostracon: 6th Century BCE, references YHWH, and the Jerusalem temple.

Hezekiah's Tunnel: This tunnel was built by Hezekiah to bring water into Jerusalem (2 Kings 20:20). It still exists today. There is even an inscription (see insert) in the tunnel that was put there by the tunnel's builders nearly three thousand years ago.

68

The Ossuary of Caiaphas: This "bone box" belonged to Caiaphas, the high priest who judged Jesus.

The Ossuary of James: This "bone box" has been associated with James the brother of Jesus. Although debated, key experts argue for its authenticity. World renowned paleographer Ada Yardeni famously quipped, "If this is a forgery, I quit."

The Pontius Pilate inscription: This inscription confirms the biblical account of Pilate, his title and the time and location in which he served.

The Sea of Galilee boat: This first century fishing boat is the type of boat Jesus preached from and traveled in and may have even been one he sailed in.

The archeological evidence for the historicity of the Bible.

The archeological finds described in this lesson are just a few exciting examples of the historical reliability of the Bible. There are many more great archeological finds that support the accuracy of Scripture and there are new ones being found all the time.

What do you think of the archeological evidence?

Norm Geisler summarizes the archeological evidence stating, "While thousands of finds from the ancient world support in broad outline and often in detail the biblical picture, not one incontrovertible find has ever contradicted the Bible."[8] Skeptics will try to refute the historical accuracy of scripture but they have been proven wrong time and again. The historical accuracy of the Bible is unparalleled.

There are also fantastical claims that you should not gullibly repeat. You may have seen pictures or heard stories of Egyptian chariot wheels in the Red Sea, giant skeletons, or other fantastical finds; these are a total hoaxes. Be careful not to gullibly repeat things there is no evidence for.

How can you guard from repeating false claims in the future?

You can, however, rest assured: archeology keeps confirming the biblical accounts and the Bible is historically accurate!

 J. Warner Wallace is a cold case homicide detective that used to be an atheist. He applied the same techniques he had used as a detective to the evidence concerning the historical reliability of the Gospel accounts. He determined the Gospels were historically accurate. In 1996, he became a follower of Jesus and is now a world-renowned Christian apologist. Find out more about him at coldcasechristianity.com.

Conclusion

The Bible claims to be historically true. Jesus claimed that people, places, and events in the Bible were historically true. Archeology continues to demonstrate the historical reliability of the Bible. Skeptics have often tried to erode the historical reliability of the Bible but the Bible has stood the test of time and proved true again and again.

Memorize some of the archeological evidence that was presented in this section. Share it with your skeptical friends. Be ready to bring some of these issues up when you encounter questions about the Bible's reliability in evangelistic conversations. Finally, remind yourself of these truths when you face doubt too. The Bible is archeologically accurate and trustworthy.

Activity: List 3 archeological finds described in this lesson that you'll commit to memory and use in apologetical conversations (note: avoid those that were said to be questionable):

1.

2.

3.

Book suggestions:

The Popular Handbook of Archaeology and the Bible: Discoveries That Confirm the Reliability of Scripture by Holden and Geisler.

Jesus and His World: The Archaeological Evidence by Craig Evans

[1] Merrill, Rooker, and Grisanti, The World and the Word: An Introduction to the Old Testament, [2] http://www.biblicalarchaeology.org/daily/people-cultures-in-the-bible/people-in-the-bible/50-people-in-the-bible-confirmed-archeologically/, [3] http://www.ritmeyer.com/2012/01/03/fiscal-bulla-found-in-jerusalem/, [4] Craig Keener, Acts: An Exegetical Commentary: Introduction and 1:1-2:47, p. 220, [5] Richard Bauckham, Jesus and the Eyewitnesses: The Gospels as Eyewitness Testimony 2nd Edition. [6] Collins and Scott, Discovering the City of Sodom: The Fascinating, True Account of the Discovery of the Old Testament's Most Infamous City. [7] http://popular-archaeology.com/issue/summer-2016/article/ancient-james-ossuary-and-jehoash-tablet-inscriptions-may-be-authentic-say-experts, [8] Norm Geisler, The Baker Encyclopedia of Christian Apologetics, p. 52

Learn This

1) Please write out the BEST FACTS and TALL TALES acronyms (see p. 114).

The BEST acronym (reasons to believe in God).
B - The **B**_____ of the universe points to God.
E - The **E**_____ of the universe points to God.
S - **S**_____ and morality point to God.
T - The **T**_____ about Jesus points to God.

The FACTS acronym (reasons to trust the Bible).
F - The Bible **F**_____ the future.
A - The Bible is **A**_____ accurate.
C - The Bible is **C**_____.
T - The Bible has been **T**_____ correctly.
S - The Bible is **S**_____ accurate.

The TALL acronym (reasons to reject other worldviews).
T - Other worldviews are **T**_____ incoherent.
A - Other worldviews make **A**_____ truth claims.
L - Other worldviews **L**_____ evidence and require a "leap of faith."
L - Other worldviews **L**_____ of power to change lives.

The TALES acronym (reasons to dismiss evolution).
T - The **T**_____ species are missing.
A - The **A**_____ of evolution is insufficient.
L - **L**_____ can't arise from non-life.
E - The **E**_____ of information and design is naturalistically inexplicable.
S - The **S**_____ of the universe from nothing is too.

2) How can you put what you learned in this lesson into practice when you deal with doubt?

3) How can you put what you learned in this lesson into practice when you defend your faith?

8
The Bible is Coherent

C - The Bible is Coherent.

Jesus claimed to be the truth and insisted that everyone on the side of truth would listen to Him (Jn. 14:6, 18:37). Jesus' statements demand that His words and the rest of scripture be respected as truth. Thankfully, the Bible is truthful and coherent and we can trust Jesus on this point.

The Bible is coherent and contradiction free. The Bible corresponds with reality. Much has been made of the supposed contradictions in the Bible but these are easily cleared up with careful analysis. Most of these supposed contradictions arise due to our modern misunderstanding of the text. There are good answers for any contradictions the skeptic might bring up.

The Bible corresponds with reality.

The Bible is internally coherent. The Bible manages to teach us on countless subjects without contradiction or error.

The Bible is externally coherent. It accurately reflects the reality of the universe around us and the history that brought us to this point.

The Bible is personally coherent. It accurately describes the human condition and a relevant solution.

> *Why must the Bible be coherent in these three areas (internally, externally, and personally)?*

The Bible is internally coherent.

Although written by 44 different people over the course of two millennia, it is internally coherent. Its diverse authors agree! Although skeptics often accuse the Bible of being riddled with errors, a careful examination shows this isn't the case.

Some critics cite scribal errors. CARM, a great apologetics resource, explains different types of scribal errors including dittography (writing twice what should have been written once), fission (improperly dividing one word into two words), fusion (combining the last letter of one word with the first letter of the next word), haplography (writing once what should have been written twice), homophony (writing a word with a different meaning for another word when both words have the exact same pronunciation), and metathesis (an improper exchange in the order of letters).[1] These do not detract from the inerrancy of scripture (more later). Cultural misunderstandings account for other accusations of error.

Dr. Mike Licona has demonstrated how many of the supposed contradictions in the New Testament were really just literary conventions associated with the Greco-Roman biography writing style.[2] No one would think your team murdered its opponents if you claimed they slaughtered them in a recent game. That's a figure of speech modern listeners are familiar with. There are similar expressions in scripture and these should not be read from a modern frame of reference. Reading the Bible as it was intended to be read is critical. Failing to do this will leave one with the impression of errors.

One example of this is Jesus' statement that "as Jonah was three days and three nights in the belly of a huge fish, so the Son of Man will be three days and three nights in the heart of the earth" (Matt. 12:40). Many critics have pointed out that Jesus died on a Thursday and rose on a Sunday morning; in other words, He was not in the grave three days and three nights. They fail to recognize how the people of that time spoke about time and the cultural expression we see repeated in Esther 4:16-5:1.[3]

Divergent accounts in the Gospels have confused others. For example, Matthew said one angel rolled the stone away from the tomb, Mark said that one angel spoke to the women inside the tomb, Luke said that two angels appeared to the women outside of the tomb, and John claimed two angels appeared to Mary inside of the tomb. These are not contradictory stories. They all reflect different details at different instants in time in the larger story. They are not truly contradictory (for example, whenever there are two there is always one) and actually support the credibility of scripture. Eyewitness testimony often includes different nuances that don't contradict each other but might sound confusing.

Plain ignorance explains some other types of errors. For example, some critics incorrectly claim that the Bible claims Pi equals 3.0. 1 Kings 7:23 and 2 Chronicles 4:2 describe a metal basin in Solomon's palace. It's dimensions were 10 cubits across and 30 around. This ornamental work of art was nearly perfectly circular. The Bible does not, however, say that it was a perfect circle or that Pi equals 3.

More recently, numerous news sources and even a world renowned scientific journal reported that a modern genetic analysis showed the descendants of the Canaanites were living in Lebanon. Many of these sources claimed this refuted the biblical claim that Israel had destroyed the Canaanites.[4] These sources somehow missed the fact that the Bible never said the Canaanites were destroyed. Even Jesus ministered to a Canaanite woman in Matthew 15.

Has a supposed contradiction ever bothered you; if so, which of these categories did it fall into?

The doctrine of inerrancy.

Dr. Craig Blomberg clarifies something very important: we are not Christians because of inherency, we believe inerrancy because we are Christians.[5] Our faith rests on what Jesus did for us at the Cross. That being said, the doctrine of inerrancy is defendable.

It is important to understand what inerrancy means and what that looks like. First of all, the doctrine of inerrancy claims that the Bible is inspired and given by God in its original autographs. That does not mean that every biblical fragment or manuscript in existence is flawless. Through textual criticism scholars can reconstitute the Bible as God delivered it, discovering variants in the manuscripts by comparing the thousands manuscripts that exist.

It is also important to read the Bible as it was intended to be read, not through our current cultural understandings. Learning what the biblical authors intended with what they wrote clears up many supposed contradictions.

The Bible is externally coherent.

The Bible accurately reflects the reality of the universe around us. The Bible is historically accurate and correctly describes our history. You can read more about this in chapter 7. The Bible is also coherent with the reality of the material universe

How have you noticed the Bible's correspondence with reality?

around us. Scientific statements in the Bible reveal God's fingerprints on His word. You'll learn more about this in chapter 10.

The Bible is personally coherent.

The Bible accurately describes your condition. It has been said that there are only two religions; the one that says you can get to God on your own by trying harder to do good and the one that says you can't get to God on your own and you need a Savior.

The Bible accurately diagnoses our sinful condition. It accurately defines our inability to solve our own predicament. It describes a legitimate and historically accurate solution to our problem, Christ's death and resurrection. Finally the Bible alone provides you with a relevant solution, the free gift of salvation by grace through faith (Eph. 2:8-9). Your testimony is an example of this!

The Bible is coherent when it comes to its relationship to human beings. No other book accurately describes our condition or a relevant solution.

Activity: Consider your testimony. What two words describe your life before Christ and why? Explain.

1.

2.

How did you come to know Christ?

What two words describe your new life with Christ and why? Explain.

1.

2.

Rehearse this and prepare to share your testimony in a minute or two when opportunities arise!

Conclusion

 G. K. Chesterton is one notable example of someone who attributed his faith to the coherence of Scripture. Chesterton was a British author whose works were instrumental in C. S. Lewis' conversion. His famous book *Orthodoxy* is an absolute masterpiece. Throughout his writing, he convincingly describes the coherence of Scripture and Christianity and how that confirms our faith.

The coherence of scripture is unfathomable. There is no significant question it doesn't provide answers for. There is no point in its theology or doctrine where it is contradictory. It correctly defines reality, the human condition, and the only relevant solution. The coherence of Scripture is a valuable point to share with skeptical friends and an important thing to remember when you deal with doubt.

Book suggestion:

Orthodoxy by G. K. Chesterton.

[1] https://carm.org/introduction-bible-difficulties-and-bible-contradictions, [2] http://eternityimpact.sermon.net/main/main/20817183 and http://eternityimpact.sermon.net/main/main/20817184, [3] https://carm.org/how-long-was-jesus-dead-tomb, [4] https://evolutionnews.org/2017/07/for-culturally-illiterate-science-reporters-ancient-canaanite-dna-yields-occasion-to-slap-the-bible-around/, [5] Craig Blomberg, Can We Still Believe the Bible?: An Evangelical Engagement with Contemporary Questions.

1) Please write out the BEST FACTS and TALL TALES acronyms (see p. 114).

The BEST acronym (reasons to believe in God).
B - The **B**_____ of the universe points to God.
E - The **E**_____ of the universe points to God.
S - S_____ and morality point to God.
T - The **T**_____ about Jesus points to God.

The FACTS acronym (reasons to trust the Bible).
F - The Bible **F**_____ the future.
A - The Bible is **A**_____ accurate.
C - The Bible is **C**_____.
T - The Bible has been **T**_____ correctly.
S - The Bible is **S**_____ accurate.

The TALL acronym (reasons to reject other worldviews).
T - Other worldviews are **T**_____ incoherent.
A - Other worldviews make **A**_____ truth claims.
L - Other worldviews **L**_____ evidence and require a "leap of faith."
L - Other worldviews **L**_____ of power to change lives.

The TALES acronym (reasons to dismiss evolution).
T - The **T**_____ species are missing.
A - The **A**_____ of evolution is insufficient.
L - **L**_____ can't arise from non-life.
E - The **E**_____ of information and design is naturalistically inexplicable.
S - The **S**_____ of the universe from nothing is too.

2) How can you put what you learned in this lesson into practice when you deal with doubt?

3) How can you put what you learned in this lesson into practice when you defend your faith?

9
The Bible is Translated Correctly

T - The Bible has been <u>T</u>ranslated Correctly.

Jesus clearly stated that the integrity of God's Word would be safeguarded until the end of time (Matt. 5:18). This has proven to be the case. The accurate preservation of the Bible's original text is unparalleled among ancient works.

We've all heard the statement that you can't trust the Bible because it has been translated too many times. People often try to equate the Bible with the "telephone game" not realizing the Bible's reliability. The attacks are unfounded. There are many early manuscripts allowing us to know for certain what was written. The New Testament has been described as the most reliable ancient text. You can and should trust it!

How the Bible was written.

The Bible's sixty-six books were written over nearly two thousand years by a total of forty-four authors. 2 Tim. 3:16 tells us that "All Scripture is God-breathed" and 2 Peter 1:21 tells us that the Holy Spirit inspired God's prophets with His words. Although written by men, the Bible was authored by God. The evidence we've been studying in the FACTS acronym points to the Divine inspiration of the Bible.

How the Bible was put together.

Early on, believers began formally recognizing the books that had been widely recognized as inspired from the beginning. The criteria they used included apostolicity (direct or indirect association with an apostle or prophet), orthodoxy (did the manuscript agree with what the church knew to be true), antiquity (was the manuscript traced to the beginning of the church, later fabrications, like the gnostic gospels, were rejected), and ecclesiastical usage (had the manuscript been accepted by a large portion of the Body of Christ since the early church).[1]

Early in the church's history, various councils of church leaders met to formally affirm which books met these criteria. These included the Council of Laodicea (in 363 AD), the Council of Hippo Regius (in 393 AD), and the Council of Carthage (in 397 AD).[1] A canon, or standard, of biblical books that met these criteria was assembled and passed down to us today.

How does this knowledge help you better trust the Bible?

How the Bible was preserved.

In spite of efforts by many throughout the ages (like Diocletian's order in 303 AD to burn all the scriptures in the Roman empire[1]), the Bible has been preserved remarkably for us today. The Bible has been preserved with a "power in numbers" approach. There are thousands of NT manuscripts that allow errors in any of the variants to be found through comparison.

The manuscript evidence for the Bible.

The reliability of the Old Testament was famously demonstrated by the Dead Sea scroll finds in the 1940s. There are other arguments for the reliability of the Old Testament as well.

The manuscript evidence for the New Testament is unparalleled in the ancient world.[2] There are nearly six thousand Greek manuscripts with some dating back to within a century of the original manuscripts (more manuscripts are still being found; and some of the earliest ever). The next most reliable ancient manuscript is Homer's Iliad; there are about six hundred copies, the earliest is from 500 years after the original. In spite of numerous variants within the different Greek New Testament manuscripts, the accuracy of these manuscripts has been established at 99.5%.[3]

In addition to the Greek manuscripts, there are more than 18,000 early translations of these documents that further corroborate what was written. Additionally, early church leaders quoted both the Old and New Testaments and their quotes corroborate much of the New Testament.

There are variants in some of the ancient documents. Bart Ehrman is widely recognized as the most formidable critic of the NT of our time. He claims there are as many as 400,000 variants across the thousands of NT manuscripts. Although this number is likely right, it does not erode the credibility of Scripture since the vast number of manuscripts allows these variants to be found and since none of these variants affects any Christian doctrine. Even Ehrman admits this.[4]

What does Ehrman's admission about the soundness of biblical doctrine tell you?

Also remember that variants don't detract from the doctrine of inerrancy, which states that God gave us His Word inerrantly, not that no error has ever been made in any translation or copy of the Bible. Biblical scholars are committed to sifting through thousands of manuscripts to find any errors that have been made in any of those copies so that we can reconstruct the original text as it was delivered to us by God. None of these variants contradicts Christian doctrine. They also don't prevent us from knowing what was originally written. Remember, the New Testament accuracy stands at 99.5%[3] and no variant affects Christian doctrine.[4]

We can be confident of the original message of Scripture. It is probably a good thing that we don't have the original manuscripts. Making changes in these would be easier than changing thousands of manuscripts. Similarly, there would be a tendency to idolize them. God has sovereignly preserved His word through a vast number of manuscript copies!

Why the telephone game accusation doesn't work.

When kids play the telephone game, one person will whisper a phrase to another that then evolves as it is whispered from person to person. Without a record of what was originally spoken, the original statement would be lost. However, if the original statement was written and preserved the meaning would not be lost regardless of any future misstatements. The Bible has been written and preserved for us!

The telephone game accusation does't work because anyone can look at the Hebrew text of the Old Testament and the Greek text of the New Testament to see what was originally written. There are numerous resources, both in print and online that make it easy for anyone to do this. One great site that allows you to do this is blueletterbible.org.

What are the differences between the telephone game and the biblical manuscripts?

The validity of most modern translations.

There are bad translations. For example, the Jehovah's Witnesses have changed hundreds of verses to support their cult's views. Fortunately, most modern translations accurately translate the text of the Bible. Some do a good job of translating the Bible in a word-for-word way. The New American Standard is an example of this. Others do a good job of giving a thought-for-thought translation. The Living Bible is an example of this. Some do a good job of getting a balance between the two. The New International Version is an example of this. Paraphrases, like the Message, are not true translations. If you stick with mainstream translations that you find in Christian bookstores you'll be just fine.

What is your favorite translation and why?

Conclusion

Josh McDowell is an example of an atheist that came to faith in Christ because he "had to admit that the Old and New Testament documents were some of the most reliable writings in all of antiquity."[5] He added, "And if they were reliable, what about this man Jesus, whom I had dismissed as a mere carpenter? I had to admit that Jesus Christ was more than a carpenter. He was all He claimed to be."[5]

The Bible has been inspired by God and the text of the Bible has been preserved in a way that no other ancient text has. Because of this, you can be confident that what you read in Scripture is what was originally written. Many people quote the incorrect "it's been translated too many times to trust it" attack since they've never been presented with the evidence for the trustworthiness of Scripture. Share this evidence with them and remind yourself of it too when you face doubt.

Book suggestion:

Can We Still Believe the Bible?: An Evangelical Engagement with Contemporary Questions by Craig Blomberg.

[1] The Cradle the Cross and the Crown, [2] Josh McDowell, Evidence that Demands a Verdict, [3] Daniel Wallace, The Majority Text and the Original Text: Are they Identical, p. 157-158, [4] Craig Blomberg, Can We Still Believe the Bible?: An Evangelical Engagement with Contemporary Questions, p. 27. [5] Josh McDowell, https://www.cru.org/how-to-know-god/my-story-a-life-changed/my-story-josh-mcdowell.html.

1) Please write out the BEST FACTS and TALL TALES acronyms (see p. 114).

(see p. 114)

The BEST acronym (reasons to believe in God).

B - The **B**_____ of the universe points to God.

E - The **E**_____ of the universe points to God.

S - **S**_____ and morality point to God.

T - The **T**_____ about Jesus points to God.

The FACTS acronym (reasons to trust the Bible).

F - The Bible **F**_____ the future.

A - The Bible is **A**_____ accurate.

C - The Bible is **C**_____.

T - The Bible has been **T**_____ correctly.

S - The Bible is **S**_____ accurate.

The TALL acronym (reasons to reject other worldviews).

T - Other worldviews are **T**_____ incoherent.

A - Other worldviews make **A**_____ truth claims.

L - Other worldviews **L**_____ evidence and require a "leap of faith."

L - Other worldviews **L**_____ of power to change lives.

The TALES acronym (reasons to dismiss evolution).

T - The **T**_____ species are missing.

A - The **A**_____ of evolution is insufficient.

L - **L**_____ can't arise from non-life.

E - The **E**_____ of information and design is naturalistically inexplicable.

S - The **S**_____ of the universe from nothing is too.

2) How can you put what you learned in this lesson into practice when you deal with doubt?

3) How can you put what you learned in this lesson into practice when you defend your faith?

10
The Bible is Scientifically Accurate

S - The Bible is <u>S</u>cientifically Accurate.

Jesus affirmed God as Creator of the universe (Mk. 10:6). He also claimed to be God (Jn. 5:18, 8:58) and Scripture tells us He is the God of creation (Jn. 1:1-3). Jesus also claimed to be the truth (Jn. 14:6). This serves as Jesus' affirmation of the truthfulness of Scripture on matters of God's creation.

The Bible is not a science textbook but its numerous scientific pronouncements show yet again the fingerprints of God. Many scientific realities were written in scripture thousands of years before science caught up. The skeptic can't just ignore these. These are yet another piece of the comprehensive case for the Christian faith.

Scientific but not a science text book.

The Bible includes scientific statements but it is not necessarily thorough on all scientific topics. Some statements seem to be unscientific. These need to be read as they were intended to be understood. For example, the four corners of the earth (Rev. 20:8) does not imply that the earth is a cube (Is. 40:22 already settled that). Rather, it is talking about every part of the earth, from the North, South, East, and West. There are also statements that are boldly stated and clearly scientific (ex. the beginning of the universe, Gen. 1:1) and some that are vague but seem to imply a scientific reality (ex. earth's molten outer core, Job.28:5). Although not a comprehensive scientific textbook, the Bible does describe numerous features of the universe that science has confirmed.

General revelation and Divine revelation.

Biblical scholars have long differentiated between General revelation and Divine revelation. General revelation is what can be known about God from creation alone. A lot can be known about God simply by observing the universe He has created (Rom. 1:20). However, there is a lot about God that can only be revealed through His Divine revelation, the Bible.

How do you think the Bible and science work in harmony?

Is there a conflict between the Bible and science? No! Although the common narrative is that there is, reality tells us that there is amazing agreement between the two. General revelation and Divine revelation will never be in conflict. If a supposed conflict exists, it is always due to a misunderstanding of one or the other. The Bible accurately describes the universe around us.

A few examples of scientific statements in the Bible.

Creation: Genesis 1:1 says, "In the beginning God created the heavens and the earth." The beginning of the universe was not even recognized by science until the twentieth century. It is now confirmed beyond any reasonable doubt. The Bible got this right in its very first verse. Science took another 4,000 years to figure this out.

Light: Ps. 104:2 says, "He wraps himself in light as with a garment." This verse correctly describes the bendable nature of light. This is something Einstein predicted and science has since confirmed.

The expansion of the universe: Ps. 104:2 continues, "he stretches out the heavens." This continuing action of stretching out the heavens, the biblical word for the universe, is repeated again in Job 9:8, 26:7, Is. 40:22, and Zec. 12:1. This wasn't confirmed by science until the 1920's when Hubble discovered it.

The circle of the earth: Is. 40:22, which we previously mentioned concerning the expansion of the universe, also describes the "circle" of the earth. Many have noticed how this corroborates the spherical nature of the earth.

The 2nd law of thermodynamics (entropy): Ps. 102:26 says the heavens and the earth "will all wear out like a garment." Heb. 1:11 and Isa 51:6 echo this statement. Science didn't learn this until the 19th century.

General Relativity: Ps. 90:4 and 2 Peter 3:8 both assert that time can be viewed or experienced in different ways by different observers. Ps. 90:4 states, "For a thousand years in your sight are like a day that has just gone by, or like a watch in the night." This actually describes the possibility of one segment of time being experienced either as a millennium, as a day, or as a few hours. Einstein's theory of General Relativity predicted this and science confirms this fascinating future of time as well.

Radioactive decay: 2 Peter 3:10 says that the elements "elements will be destroyed by fire" in a way that will have disastrous effects. 2 Peter 3:12 reiterates that stating again that "the elements will melt in the heat." The Greek word used here for elements is stoicheion (στοιχεῖον) and it meant any first thing, from which the others belonging to some series or composite whole take their rise, an element, a first principal.[1] Scripture accurately described the destructive decomposition of elements and atoms in the first century (science confirmed this in the 19th century).

Earth's foundation: Job 26:7 tells us that earth's foundation is hung on nothing. This is striking! The Greeks attributed the earth's foundation to the mythical god

Atlas while other worldviews picked a numerous assortment of foundations. All the while the Bible described it correctly.

That weight of the air: Job 28:25 describes the "weight of the wind," something that seems to imply the mass of molecules in the air. This would have been difficult for someone 4,000 years ago to predict. Modern chemistry has confirmed the mass of the gasses that constitute the air we breathe.

Hydrologic cycles. Ps. 135:7, Ec. 1:7, and Job 36:27-29 are just a few of the references that describe hydrologic cycles.

Atmospheric jet streams: Ecc. 1:6 seems to describe atmospheric jet streams.

Ocean springs: Hydrothermic vents or springs in the oceans are described in Gen. 7:11 and Job. 38:16.

Biology: Gen. 1:11-12, 21, 25 describe the biological law that like begets like.

Genetics confirms that all humans come from one female ancestor, who is often referred to as Mitochodrial Eve, and that all males come from one male ancestor, who is often referred to as Y-chromosomal Adam. This is consistent with scripture.

Many biblical scholars have long assumed that God's curse on the serpent, in Genesis 3:14, implied that snakes originally had legs. This seemed like a stretched harmonization to many. Just recently, scientists discovered *Tetrapodophis amplectus*, what they believe was a four legged snake! Here's a picture of it. Whether this is fossil evidence of the curse or not, it surely doesn't contradict the Bible.

Tetrapodophis' hind legs

Another biological surprise is the *Archaeopteryx*, a bird with some reptile characteristics. Although some insist this is a missing link between birds and reptiles, it was really one that was created uniquely by God and that is even described in the Bible. Leviticus 11:18 describes *Tanshemeth* (Strong's number 08580) as a bird (translated as "white owl") while Leviticus 11:30 includes it in a list of reptiles (translated as "chameleon")! There is no other creature like this in the fossil record and there is no other creature like this in scripture.[2]

Earth's molten outer core: Job.28:5 seems to describe earth's molten outer core. This may or may not be the case. You can read it and decide for yourself.

A Comprehensive Case.

These are just some of the scientific statements included in scripture. As you noticed, some are stronger than others. If these were the only reasons to believe the Bible, they'd be worth considering. Thankfully, the comprehensive case for the Bible is much greater and this is just one of the arguments for it.

Conclusion

Isaac Newton is one of the most famous scientists of all time who was also a committed believer. He recognized that God was revealed in nature and necessary as its cause. He wrote, "Gravity explains the motions of the planets, but it cannot explain who set the planets in motion. God governs all things and knows all that is or can be done."[3]

Science can't prove God. It can, however, point to Him. In fact, science itself would not be possible without the predictability of a universe governed by God. The Bible isn't a scientific textbook but it does have scientific statements that show God's fingerprints on His word. Share some of these scientific statements and other arguments, like the cosmological argument and the design argument to show how science demonstrates the need for God. When you struggle with doubt, remind yourself of these fascinating examples of science in the Bible.

> *What are your thoughts on science and the Bible?*

Book suggestion:

God's Undertaker: Has Science Buried God by John Lennox.

[1] Stoicheion, Strong's Number: 4747, http://classic.studylight.org, [2] Gerald Schroeder, The Science of God, p. 101. [3] Isaac Newton: Inventor, Scientist and Teacher.

Learn This

1) Please write out the BEST FACTS and TALL TALES acronyms (see p. 114).

The BEST acronym (reasons to believe in God).
B - The **B**_____ of the universe points to God.
E - The **E**_____ of the universe points to God.
S - **S**_____ and morality point to God.
T - The **T**_____ about Jesus points to God.

The FACTS acronym (reasons to trust the Bible).
F - The Bible **F**_____ the future.
A - The Bible is **A**_____ accurate.
C - The Bible is **C**_____.
T - The Bible has been **T**_____ correctly.
S - The Bible is **S**_____ accurate.

The TALL acronym (reasons to reject other worldviews).
T - Other worldviews are **T**_____ incoherent.
A - Other worldviews make **A**_____ truth claims.
L - Other worldviews **L**_____ evidence and require a "leap of faith."
L - Other worldviews **L**_____ of power to change lives.

The TALES acronym (reasons to dismiss evolution).
T - The **T**_____ species are missing.
A - The **A**_____ of evolution is insufficient.
L - **L**_____ can't arise from non-life.
E - The **E**_____ of information and design is naturalistically inexplicable.
S - The **S**_____ of the universe from nothing is too.

2) How can you put what you learned in this lesson into practice when you deal with doubt?

3) How can you put what you learned in this lesson into practice when you defend your faith?

11
Reasons to Reject other Worldviews

The TALL acronym - Reasons to reject other worldviews.

Jesus was adamant that he alone was the way, the truth, and the life (Jn. 14:6) and that other candidates "were thieves and robbers" (Jn. 10:8). Jesus claimed to be the only way. Although troubling to many, truth is always exclusive. Two plus two always equals four. Jesus' exclusive claims are not intended to alienate people but to explain to them the truth of reality so they can experience what only Jesus offers: salvation by grace and through faith. Jesus really is the only way.

This lesson will give a very brief overview of some of the reasons Christians can confidently reject other worldviews. Remember, this is what is called negative apologetics and it shouldn't be your focus. If you have to give an answer for why you don't believe other faiths, be careful to respectfully use these arguments.

The TALL acronym.

The TALL acronym describes why other religious perspectives are lacking. Remember to be respectful as you engage people from other faiths. Other religious perspectives fall short because of their:

How can you respectfully reach out to friends of other faiths?

T – Theological incoherence: Other religious perspectives are theologically incoherent. They are self contradictory. This criticism is often leveled at Christianity as well and you can find good answers to that in the FACTS acronym. Such contradictions include references to Jesus as both God and the brother of Satan, references to salvation by grace and works, the concept of reincarnation (which is logically invalid) and other incoherencies too numerous to elaborate on here. The bottom line, true Christianity is coherent while other religious perspectives are riddled with inconsistencies.

A few examples of this in other faiths illustrate this point. Animism and tribal religions are based in myth and are disconnected from reality. Buddhism and Hinduism believe in reincarnation, which assumes an infinite regress into the past, something that is impossible.[1] Even, if for the sake of argument, we granted it, why hasn't moksha and perfection been attained after an infinite amount of time?[2] Islam claims that "Whoever kills a soul … it is as if he had slain mankind entirely" (Quran 5:32) yet commands adherents to behead non-Muslims (Quran 8:12) and "slay the idolaters wherever you find them" (9:5), even those of the book, Christians and Jews (9:29). The book of Mormon has numerous conflicts with scripture (like claiming Jesus was born in Jerusalem and that there will be marriage in heaven) and has had thousands of revisions and corrections. Atheism argued for God's non-existence, which is an absolute negation, a fallacy. In contrast, the Bible is different: It is internally coherent, externally coherent, and personally coherent.

A - Ambiguous truth claims: Religions other than Christianity involve ambiguous truth claims which undermine their authority. Some might say that certain things were right but are now wrong (ex. polygamy) or vice versa while others might have conflicting perspectives (ex. desire causes all evil yet one must desire to overcome evil). Fortunately, the Bible makes clear truth claims and avoids the ambiguity prevalent in many other religious perspectives.

Animism is inherently ambiguous. Buddhism insists that desire is the root of all suffering yet insists that to overcome suffering, one must desire to follow the eight fold path. Islam claims that man was created from nothing (Sura 19:67), from dust (Sura 30:20), from clay (Sura 15:26), from water (Sura 25:54), from a blood clot (Sura 96:1-2), and from sperm (Sura 40:67). Christian Cults are ambiguous concerning the nature of God (transcendent or one of us), the nature of Jesus (brother of Satan, Michael the Archangel, etc.), the nature of people (will be gods), marriage (eternal or not - Matt. 22), and most importantly, salvation. Atheism is no less flawed, basing its merits in science although science could never disprove the supernatural. The Bible stands alone in its clarity concerning origin, meaning, morality, and destiny.

L - Lack of evidence requiring a "leap of faith."
Most religions talk about history that isn't accurate, scientific statements that have been proven false, prophetic predictions that have not come true and a wholesale lack of evidence requiring a blind leap of faith. Christianity is quite different. The FACTS acronym will explain this in more detail. Fortunately, The Bible is supported not just by an emotional connection to a leap of faith but rather by hard evidence that supports all it says. We a take a confident step of faith not a blind leap of faith.

Why is evidence important in matters of faith?

Christianity stands alone among the world's faiths in its evidentiary perspective. Animism, Hinduism, and Buddhism don't even propose to be based in evidence. Many of the Christian cults are blatantly unhistoric. Mormonism is an example of this. There is no evidence for the people groups it claims inhabited North America, the Nephites and Lamanites, nor that Native North Americans descended from Israelites; DNA and linguistics point to Asian ancestry. No Hebrew artifacts have ever been discovered in North America nor evidence of the people, cities, wars or events in the Book of Mormon. There are many other archeological problems with the Book of Mormon as well. For example, elephants, bees, horses, other animals, certain grains and fruits, silk and steel are mentioned in the Book of Mormon but were not known in North America prior to its discovery by Europeans. Finally, atheism is assumed based on an incorrect assumption that there is not evidence for God's existence; atheists rarely even try to offer evidence for God's non-existence.

L - Lack of power to change lives. Most religions advocate just trying harder and just struggling more to achieve "perfection." They fail to realize the utter depravity of man. Malcolm Muggeridge once said, "The Depravity of man is at once the most empirically verifiable reality but at the same time the most intellectually resisted fact." Humans cannot change themselves as all world religions other than Christianity claim they must. We truly need a Savior who will change us from the inside out as the Bible claims Jesus does. Jesus not only saves us from our sin, He empowers us, through His Holy Spirit, to become the people He made us to be.

Why is the Gospel unique?

Again, other worldviews are hopelessly bankrupt here. Animism and tribal religions try to manipulate unseen and unknown forces. Buddhism yields no true hope, only and endless struggle through suffering. Hinduism requires Hindus to work their way through the caste system, hoping for eventual relief. It says nothing for the rest of humanity. Islam is works based with no true hope or guarantee of salvation. The Christian Cults are no less helpful. Atheism is based on the mirage of self-realization. Secular humanism offers not true hope. The Bible is different; Jesus really changes peoples' lives. There are countless millions who have been radically transformed by the power of the Gospel.

Remember, only reference the TALL arguments if you absolutely have to. Try to stay positive focusing on the evidence for your faith in Jesus rather than attacking others. Only bring these up to respectfully answer specific questions if needed.

Conclusion

This was a very brief introduction to four reasons Christians can reject other faiths. Jesus really did claim to be the only way to God. C. S. Lewis correctly stated that either Jesus was a liar, a lunatic, or Lord.[2] His life demonstrated he was neither a liar nor a lunatic. Every single person must consider His claim to be Lord.

 Nabeel Qureshi was a former Muslim who came to know Jesus after a long time of researching the evidence for and against both Islam and Christianity. His book *Seeking Allah, Finding Jesus* describes his journey. His third book, *No God but One: Allah or Jesus*, describes how to share the evidence for Christianity with Muslim friends. Pray for Nabeel's family as they mourn his recent loss.

When you share the broad TALL rebuttals against other faiths, be very careful to be respectful. Try to focus more on the evidence for Christianity and be very careful to keep the Gospel at the forefront. Devote time to learning more about using apologetics relate to their specific faiths. Learn to befriend and love people from other faiths that you are trying to reach out to.

Other religions are all centered on what man can do for Himself. Jesus alone offers a real solution to the human condition. Jesus alone conquered death demonstrating the authority to give us eternal life.

Book suggestion:

Jesus Among Other Gods: The Absolute Claims of the Christian Message by Ravi Zacharias.

[1] The Popular Encyclopedia of Apologetics, p. 416–417, [2] C. S. Lewis, Mere Christianity, 2014, p. 53–54.

1) Please write out the BEST FACTS and TALL TALES acronyms (see p. 114).

The BEST acronym (reasons to believe in God).
B - The **B**_____ of the universe points to God.
E - The **E**_____ of the universe points to God.
S - **S**_____ and morality point to God.
T - The **T**_____ about Jesus points to God.

The FACTS acronym (reasons to trust the Bible).
F - The Bible **F**_____ the future.
A - The Bible is **A**_____ accurate.
C - The Bible is **C**_____.
T - The Bible has been **T**_____ correctly.
S - The Bible is **S**_____ accurate.

The TALL acronym (reasons to reject other worldviews).
T - Other worldviews are **T**_____ incoherent.
A - Other worldviews make **A**_____ truth claims.
L - Other worldviews **L**_____ evidence and require a "leap of faith."
L - Other worldviews **L**_____ of power to change lives.

The TALES acronym (reasons to dismiss evolution).
T - The **T**_____ species are missing.
A - The **A**_____ of evolution is insufficient.
L - **L**_____ can't arise from non-life.
E - The **E**_____ of information and design is naturalistically inexplicable.
S - The **S**_____ of the universe from nothing is too.

2) How can you put what you learned in this lesson into practice when you deal with doubt?

3) How can you put what you learned in this lesson into practice when you defend your faith?

12 Reasons to Reject Evolution & Atheism

The TALES acronym - Reasons to Reject Evolution and Atheism.

Jesus clearly described a Creator and His role in creation (Mk. 10:6). Scripture is quite clear that Jesus is God, the creator of this universe (Jn. 1:1-3, Col. 1:15-17). God created this universe and it is important that Christians learn how to defend that position and use it in evangelism.

Frame this debate right.

Even if you could prove evolution, our faith would not be shattered. There are evangelical Christians who believe God created the universe through natural processes that He ordained. Theistic evolution is bad science and bad theology (more on that in a minute). Just remember that evolution doesn't prove atheism.

Evolution typically shouldn't be the tip of your apologetical spear. Evolution should be addressed if someone thinks it is a barrier to faith. You probably don't need to focus on it if they are ready to trust Christ where they are at. You could lead them to Christ and then address the issue of evolution in discipleship.

Why should you focus more on the Gospel than disproving evolution?

The TALES acronym.

The TALES acronym includes 5 arguments against atheistic evolution and metaphysical naturalism. You probably won't want to get to stuck in these arguments if you aren't well versed in the science. Here are a few short arguments against evolution.

T – Transitional species are missing. If evolution were true, it would have to be evidenced in the fossil record. It is not. Stephen Jay Gould famously admitted, "All paleontologists know that the fossil record contains precious little in the way of intermediate forms; transitions between major groups are characteristically abrupt."[1] Even Darwin admitted this would be troublesome for his theory. Unfortunately for the theory of evolution, a fossil record full of intermediate species is non-existent.

A - Apparatus of evolution is insufficient. The proposed mechanism of evolution, natural selection working on gradual mutations, has never been supported by the evidence. Positive mutations are rare and they only decrease genetic information and natural selection cannot add any information. This leaves the theory with no valid mechanism relegating it to nothing more than a "just so story." Stephen J. Gould recognized this calling the theory of evolution by gradual mutation "... effectively dead despite its persistence as textbook orthodoxy."[2] He was, of course still an evolutionist, just willing to state the facts the way the were (he attempted to develop his own version of the theory called Punctuated Equilibrium). Without a viable, reproducible mechanism the theory falls apart.

L - Life can't arise from non-life. If naturalism were true, evolution would have to account for a naturalistic start for life. It does not. A living cell is far more complex than a few organic molecules. Go ahead and believe it when you actually see it. Until then, you can be confident that life is far too complex to come from non-life.

E - Existence of information and design. The building blocks of life (RNA and DNA) are much more than chemical structures, they are information laden blueprints for all of life. The information they hold, along with the incredible fine tuning of this universe all point to an intelligent designer. Information and design never come from any source other than intelligence (see lesson 3).

S - Start of the universe from nothing. The beginning of the universe from nothing is now a commonly accepted, scientifically confirmed reality. Science cannot give a naturalistic explanation for this and naturalism, atheism and evolution are left without a leg to stand on. You can refer back to lesson 2 for more on this.

What about theistic evolution?

Evolution is bad science and we shouldn't incorporate that into our faith. Theistic evolution is also off base theologically and doctrinally. It is a stretched harmonization that ends up being bad science and bad theology. Many people who adopt theistic evolution seem to be focused on the praise of men, wanting to fit in with the prevailing myth of origins of our time. At the end of the day, evolution is also the foundation of an atheistic paradigm that has done so much bad around the world. Christians should be wary of adopting a theistic view of evolution.

Note: Don't confuse old-earth creationists with theistic evolutionists. They are different. An old earth perspective does not necessarily affirm evolution. Old-earth creationists believe in creation and agree that evolution is false.

Conclusion

 David Berlinsky is a philosopher, mathematician, biochemist and renowned intellectual who has publicly denied the possibility of naturalistic evolution. Although not a Christian, he has been intellectually honest enough to expose the fraudulent claims of Darwinian evolution. He is is a senior fellow at the Discovery Institute's Center for Science and Culture.

Atheistic evolution is often a smoke screen that is used to substantiate people's ulterior motives for rejecting God (people usually turn to atheism for hedonistic reasons not intellectual ones). Most of the people that reject Christ on account of evolution have no real knowledge of the theory (nor the evidence for Christianity).

How can you tell if people are using evolution as a smoke screen?

The modern commitment to evolution is often associated with a conflict between faith and science. That conflict, like evolution, is a myth. For more on that, read *God's Undertaker* by John Lennox. Science and the Bible are not at odds!

As with the TALL acronym, use the TALES acronym arguments sparingly but be ready to refer to them when needed. If you encounter the issue of evolution in the course of an evangelistic conversation, be ready to share the TALES acronym in a respectful way. If you struggle with doubt in this area, remind yourself of these arguments.

Book suggestion:

I don't Have Enough Faith to be an Atheist by Geisler and Turek.

[1] Natural History, Vol LXXXVI (6), June-July, 1977, [2] Paleobiology, Vol.6, 1980, p.120.

Learn This

1) Please write out the BEST FACTS and TALL TALES acronyms (see p. 114).

The BEST acronym (reasons to believe in God).
B - The **B**_____ of the universe points to God.
E - The **E**_____ of the universe points to God.
S - **S**_____ and morality point to God.
T - The **T**_____ about Jesus points to God.

The FACTS acronym (reasons to trust the Bible).
F - The Bible **F**_____ the future.
A - The Bible is **A**_____ accurate.
C - The Bible is **C**_____.
T - The Bible has been **T**_____ correctly.
S - The Bible is **S**_____ accurate.

The TALL acronym (reasons to reject other worldviews).
T - Other worldviews are **T**_____ incoherent.
A - Other worldviews make **A**_____ truth claims.
L - Other worldviews **L**_____ evidence and require a "leap of faith."
L - Other worldviews **L**_____ of power to change lives.

The TALES acronym (reasons to dismiss evolution).
T - The **T**_____ species are missing.
A - The **A**_____ of evolution is insufficient.
L - **L**_____ can't arise from non-life.
E - The **E**_____ of information and design is naturalistically inexplicable.
S - The **S**_____ of the universe from nothing is too.

2) How can you put what you learned in this lesson into practice when you deal with doubt?

3) How can you put what you learned in this lesson into practice when you defend your faith?

13 Summary

The Best Fact of all!

The BEST FACT of all is the Gospel, the exclamation on the BEST FACTS! Make sure to communicate the Gospel clearly when you do apologetics. Remember, apologetics must happen in the context of evangelism. Please check out appendix C to learn more about sharing your faith.

There is a danger in learning apologetics just for the sake of acquiring knowledge (1 Cor. 8:1, James 1:22). Make sure to grow close to God as you learn apologetics and continue sharing what you learn with those you are witnessing to and discipling. We hope this workbook has been a real resource for you. The rest of this chapter will focus on helping you process all you've learned so far.

Major take aways from this class:

Write out the BEST FACTS:

B -

E -

S -

T -

F -

A -

C -

T -

S -

Write out the TALL TALES:

T -

A -

L -

L -

T -

A -

L -

E -

S -

My action plan for using apologetics to reach others for Jesus:

Appendix A - The BEST FACTS and TALL TALES Acronyms.

The BEST acronym.

B - The Beginning of the Universe Points to God.

E - The Engineering of the Universe Points to God.

S - Standards and Morality Point to God.

T - The Truth About Jesus Points to God.

The FACTS acronym.

F - The Bible Foretells the Future.

A - The Bible is Archeologically Accurate.

C - The Bible is Coherent.

T - The Bible has been Translated Correctly.

S - The Bible is Scientifically Accurate.

The TALL acronym.

T - Other Worldviews are Theologically Incoherent.

A - Other Worldviews make Ambiguous Truth Claims.

L - Other Worldviews Lack Evidence and Require a "Leap of Faith."

L - Other Worldviews Lack of Power to Change Lives.

The TALES acronym.

T - Transitionary Species are Missing.

A - Apparatus of Evolution is Insufficient.

L - Life can't Arise from Non-Life.

E - Existence of Information and Design.

S - Start of the Universe from Nothing.

Appendix B - Suggested Resources

Apologetics Sites: crossexamined.org, askdrbrown.org, coldcasechristianity.com, garyhabermas.com, reasonablefaith.org, carm.org, carm.org, thebestfacts.com, and godsolutionshow.com (this is the link where you can find hundreds of God Solution episodes, including interviews with the world's leading apologists).

Witnessing to Muslims: Visit http://www.nabeelqureshi.com for the best resources you'll find on this. Please read Nabeel's book No God but one: Allah or Jesus. Also check out the new CARM resource on this: https://carm.org/examining-islam

Addressing Social Issues: Visit https://askdrbrown.org for some of the best resources you'll find on this. Please read Dr. Michael Brown's books *Can you be gay and Christian* and *Outlasting the gay revolution*. Also check out Dr. Turek's book *Correct, Not Politically Correct.*

Appendix C - How to SHARE your Faith

This strategy is a simple way of remembering an effective approach to personal evangelism. SHARE stands for Supercharge, Have an expectant attitude, Ask questions, Resources and Encourage them.

First of all, where's your heart at? Matt. 12:34 - "out of the overflow of the heart the mouth speaks." If you're not sharing your faith, check your heart! Second of all, make sure you're not believing any lies. Have you believed any of these lies in the past?

- ☐ You must have the gift of evangelism.
- ☐ You must validate the Gospel and make it relevant.
- ☐ You must earn the right to be heard.
- ☐ Tracts and booklets don't work.
- ☐ Only the down and out need Jesus.
- ☐ You must make sure no one gets offended.
- ☐ Methods produce results.
- ☐ "Preach always, use words if necessary."
- ☐ Older people are stuck in their ways & unreachable.
- ☐ Most people aren't interested in spiritual issues.

Third, once you're ready to share, follow this strategy:

Supercharge: Acts 1:8 tells us that the Holy Spirit empowers believers for bold evangelism. You can walk in the power of the Holy Spirit each when you: **P**resent yourself to God, surrendering to Him (Romans 12:1-2). **O**wn up to any sin God makes you aware of and confess it to Him (1 John 1:9). **W**ant to live a Christ-like, Spirit-filled and empowered life (Matthew 5:6). **E**xperience His filling and power, claiming it by faith alone through prayer

(James 1:6-7, 1 John 5:14-15). **R**ely on Him, taking steps of faith trusting Him to do what only He can (2 Cor. 5:7). Before witnessing, consciously ask God to fill you with His Holy Spirit, empowering you to witness with His power and authority. Pray for those you will share with (remember the "Divine Order"). Then step out, supercharged with His power, trusting Him alone.

Have an expectant attitude: Look for opportunities and expect God to use you in great ways! Do not share your faith with a "no one will be interested, no one will respond, no one wants to hear this" attitude. An expectant attitude is imperative in evangelism. Go out excited to see all God will do! Your attitude will effect your willingness to obey God, the frequency with which you obey Him, the way you come across to those you share with and every other aspect of evangelism. Don't let a lack of results, opposition to your efforts or any other circumstances quell your enthusiasm. Determine today to share your faith with a joyful and expectant attitude taking the "initiative to share Christ in the power of the Holy Spirit and leaving the results to God."

Ask questions: You can transition any conversation to the Gospel, in simple and non-awkward ways, and questions are the key to doing that! Think of a few conversation starting questions you could use to get into conversations with people. Then, think of good questions that can transition to a conversation about Christ. A great example is, "What's been your experience with Christianity?" Learn to carefully, authentically and genuinely listen to people's answers, as good listening will help you find conversational transition points and build bridges with those you want to share the Good News with. It is vitally important that you make creative questions and thoughtful listening key components of your evangelism strategy. Remember Keith Davies' 3 Modes and 4 Sound Barriers.

Resources: Use resources that will help you confidently share your faith and train the next generation of people you're discipling to as well. We call these transferable resources. A great example is the KGP (Knowing God Personally) booklet, available from crupress.com. Gospel presentations like this are conversational tools that help millions of people each year put their faith in Christ. Don't shun such powerful and transferable tools, just learn how to use them in relational and non-awkward ways.

The most important thing about resources is presenting a complete description of the Gospel and an opportunity to respond. Good resources do this. It is critical that you share God's love for the person you are witnessing to. Jesus included this in His Gospel message (Jn. 3:16). You must also adequately explain the sin problem. Until someone understands that, they won't see the need for forgiveness. Especially in this day and age, where sin has been nearly completely written off, it is necessary that the person come to understand how their selfishness and imperfection have separated them from our perfectly loving God. They must also understand that sin separates us from God now, and left unmitigated, it will separate us from Him for eternity. Once the sin issue is understood, people must hear of God's only solution for that dilemma, Jesus and his payment for our sins on the cross. Finally, they must realize that they have a choice to make, to believe in Jesus, receiving His gift of salvation, or to reject Him and all that He offers.

Salvation is by grace and through faith alone. If someone is ready to believe in Jesus, you could encourage them to prayerfully begin this new relationship. A prayer won't save them; God's grace saves us and our faith, not our works, enables us to access what He has done for us. A prayer can be a helpful step that demonstrates one's faith in a way that they will always remember. You could lead them in a prayer that goes something like this:

"Jesus, I know you are who you say you are and that you died on the cross for my sins. I believe you rose again to give me new life. I ask you to come into my life as my Savior and Lord. Please make me the kind of person you want me to be."

That's not a silly prayer or a magic button but a way of demonstrating their faith in Christ.

Every Gospel presentation should include these fundamentals and most good resources will.

As you use resources, be up front with those you talk to about what you're doing. For example, if you're using a survey, mention that it is a spiritual interest survey and that you are a part of a Christian group trying to survey people. Don't trick people into listening to a Gospel presentation. Nobody likes the bait and switch technique. Be honest about what you're up to and respect their choice to listen or not.

Encourage People! Be ready to implement a follow-up plan right away. Whether someone puts their trust in Christ or is interested in hearing more, plan to meet up with them again to encourage them towards Christ. Get their contact information before leaving and don't delay in setting up a follow-up appointment. It is a shame how many hungry seekers are never followed up with and it is just as tragic when new believers are not discipled. Don't make either of these mistakes!

So there you have it, the SHARE acronym. If you will supercharge before witnessing, going out in the power of the Holy Spirit rather than trusting your own abilities, you will see fruit in evangelism. If you have an expectant attitude, you'll have tremendous joy in witnessing and will see God use you in greater ways than you can imagine. If you learn to ask questions in evangelistic conversations, you'll find yourself transitioning all sorts of conversations to the Gospel. If you add resources to all that you'll be powerfully equipped to share your faith anytime and anywhere with anyone. Finally, if you encourage those you share with, following up with those who are interested and discipling those who put their trust in Christ, you will see a constant flow of new believers flowing from your ministry.

Appendix D - Answering the Problem of Evil

The problem of evil, pain and suffering goes back millennia and it is one of the foremost objections the Christian apologist will encounter. The basic accusation is that a good, all-powerful God would eliminate suffering but since suffering exists, He is either not all-powerful or not good. Here we'll give you a few basic tools for addressing this issue.

First of all, everyone has to answer the question of the problem of evil. Atheists hold evil as evidence of God's non-existence but fail to realize that outside of an objective moral standard, there is no real good or evil (remember the moral argument for God's existence from lesson 4). Other non-Christian worldviews are equally unable to answer the question. Christianity offers a coherent answer and hope in the midst of pain and suffering.

Just like darkness is the absence of light, evil is the failure to measure up to who God is and His standard of right and wrong. The Bible calls this sin. God created a universe with people with free will and the potential for sin and evil, but He did not create evil. God created us for relationship with Him and gave us the freedom to choose to follow Him or not. Not following Him results in evil. Sin is the cause of all the moral evil on the planet. Things like theft, rape, and murder are sin. Sin is also the original cause of all natural evil; diseases, natural disasters, and the like are a consequence of humanity's sin and a universe that is now in decay. Additionally, Satan is real and is an architect of untold evil (Jn. 10:10). God does not cause evil, sinful beings do when they disobey God.

Although God does not cause evil, He can allow certain expressions of it in order to bring about a greater eternal good. God can allow evil to demonstrate the urgency of salvation, to highlight the reality that decisions have consequences, to get people's attention, because he is patiently waiting for people, both perpetrators and victims of evil, to find him, and for other reasons. As Christians, we also realize that justice will prevail! All evil will be dealt with, either at the Cross or in hell. All evil will be punished.

As believers we have hope in the midst of suffering. Romans 8:28 promises that God will turn evil and pain around for the believer's good and God's purposes. Additionally, we know God is working towards an eternal purpose that transcends all our present suffering. If God could allow temporary suffering to bring more people into eternity with Him, why wouldn't He? A tapestry analogy has been used to illustrate this. From one side, a tapestry can look like a tangled mess, while from the other side, it is seen as a beautiful work of art. From eternity, we will see why God allowed the evil he allowed on this planet and we will see the beautiful tapestry of His work in history.

Everyone has been hurt and everyone will be hurt again. It is natural to ask "why" questions when we encounter pain and suffering. If someone brings up the problem of evil as an intellectual rebuttal of your faith, feel free to walk them through the arguments we just shared. However, if someone brings this up because they are struggling with doubt because of pain they have experienced, realize you'll need to approach this a little differently.

Sometimes these apologetical answers can fall short of addressing the pain hurting people are experiencing. When you encounter someone who is wrestling with the problem of evil, pain, and suffering in a personal way, be careful to approach the problem with this in mind. Don't offer an intellectual response that fails to address someone's heart needs. Reach out to the hurting, mourn with them, serve them, sympathize with them, and love them. Focus on the hope available in Christ while they are processing their pain.

If you remember these points you'll be ready to deal with the problem of evil, pain, and suffering when you encounter it. We encourage you to read *The Problem of Pain* by C. S. Lewis and *Why Does God Allow Evil* by Clay Jones for more on this important topic.

Appendix E - 10 More Common Objections

Consider the following objections and do a little research to prepare to answer them.

1. Jesus never even existed (Read *The Case for Christ* by Lee Strobel and *The Case for the Resurrection of Jesus* by Habermas and Licona).

2. The OT God is a God of wrath (Read chapters 15 and 16 of *True Reason: Christian Responses to the Challenge of Atheism* by Gilson and Weitnauer).

3. The age of the universe (Read *Seven Days That Divide the World* by John Lennox).

4. Science and faith contradict each other (Read *God's Undertaker* by John Lennox).

5. The Bible isn't inerrant or trustworthy (Read *The Historical Reliability of the New Testament* by Craig Blomberg).

6. Miracles are impossible (Read *Miracles* by Craig Keener).

7. What about other religions and worldviews (Read *The Big Book of Christian Apologetics* by Norm Geisler)?

8. Exclusivity of Jesus (Read *Jesus Among Other Gods* by Ravi Zacharias).

9. What about LGBT issues (Read *Outlasting the Gay Revolution* by Michael Brown).

10. Who made God (Read *Who Made God* by Edgar Andrews).

About the Authors, Contributors, and Editors

 Nate Herbst (PhD) co-leads the Great Commission Alliance and co-hosts the God Solution apologetics radio show. Nate struggled with doubt for many years of his Christian life but found that there were good answers for all the questions he ever got hung up on. He has learned to trust God with various insecurities in life and ministry. He has also learned that he can't tell a joke to save his life.

 Erin Herbst (M.A) is currently re-taking pre-school through third grade as she homeschools her children. She is much sharper than Nate on most issues but she hates math. In spite of this shortcoming, she has learned that she, like any believer, can confidently share and defend her faith. She is actively involved in the Great Commission Alliance ministry that she and Nate help co-lead.

 **Grant Bresett** (M.A) works a boring government job but he's not boring! Having dabbled in atheism, mormonism, and buddhism before finding Christ, he is passionate about sharing the evidence for Jesus. He co-hosts the God Solution apologetics radio show with Nate and is heavily involved in pro-life activism. He also has master's degrees in both religion and apologetics. He is married to Jennifer who is definitely way out of his league.

 Brandon Cox is currently enrolled in Liberty University's theological seminary. He and his wife Anne have been in full time ministry since 2013. Brandon is passionate about serving Jesus and loves doing that outdoors as much as possible. He is an avid rock-climber among other outdoor hobbies. He is currently leading the campus ministry branch of the Great Commission Alliance.

 Meghan Renfro leads the graphic design section of the Great Commission Alliance. That means she's the one that came up with all the cool logos for this book. She and her husband Bennie have been on staff since 2015 and they are passionate about equipping believers for evangelism and discipleship. Meghan is certified to be a much better hunter than her husband!

 Caitlin Craft helped develop some of the application and activity sections in this workbook because she really doesn't want you to forget any of this important information. Caitlin is passionate about Jesus and ministry and hopes you get a lot out of this workbook.

51559329R00071